# ACHING FOR GREAT-NESS

"We all want more for our lives and often try to place our worth and identity in things other than God. Tanner Kalina captures that search and shows how true fulfillment and joy come from a personal relationship with our creator. *Aching for Greatness* is a relatable and engaging read that challenges us to face the questions: When will we realize the core of what we're searching for is found in Christ? When will we finally choose to give everything to God? His heartfelt story is inspiring and dares us to take our own steps toward Jesus."

**Mari Wagner**
Founder of West Coast Catholic

"Through a fresh weaving of personal testimony and ancient tradition, Tanner Kalina brings us back to the truth we all need to hear: fulfillment is only found in Christ."

**Fr. David Michael Moses**
Social media evangelist and parochial vicar of
Christ the Good Shepherd Parish in Spring, Texas

"*Aching For Greatness* is Tanner Kalina's story—but it's also mine, and it's also yours. Kalina's relatability allows the reader to find themselves in this familiar tale of the pursuit of worldly fulfillment and the inevitable emptiness that follows. Kalina challenges the reader not to give up or numb our primordial ache for greatness but to make intentional, incremental changes to our daily lives that facilitate a greater closeness with Jesus Christ, the source of fulfillment itself. Many of us struggle to take the radical leap of giving ourselves totally to Christ, but Kalina is a reassuring guide and friend throughout this inspiring book."

**Lillian Fallon**
Author of *Theology of Style: Expressing the Unique and Unrepeatable You*

# ACHING
# FOR
# GREAT-
# NESS

## DISCOVER GOD'S LOVE IN THE RESTLESS SEARCH FOR MORE

## TANNER KALINA

AVE MARIA PRESS AVE Notre Dame, Indiana

---

Founded in 1865, Ave Maria Press is a ministry of the United States Province of Holy Cross.

www.avemariapress.com

Paperback: ISBN-13 978-1-64680-342-2

E-book: ISBN-13 978-1-64680-343-9

Cover image © Maksym Kaplun / iStock / Getty Images Plus.

Cover and text design by Brianna Dombo.

Printed and bound in the United States of America.

*Library of Congress Cataloging-in-Publication Data is available.*

# CONTENTS

# FOREWORD

Have you ever wondered why you scroll and scroll to find that perfect show to stream? Or maybe why you search online or ask friends for that next great book recommendation?

I believe most of us would say that we're looking for some entertainment—perhaps something to bring us joy after a long day or a distraction to give us a break. But there's something deeper behind our search. Something more intrinsic to who we are and how we tick.

The Catholic philosopher Alasdair MacIntyre claims that each of us is "essentially a storytelling animal." He writes, "I can only answer the question, 'What am I to do?' if I can answer the prior question 'Of what story or stories do I find myself a part?'"

Deep down, all of us are looking for a story. We might not know it, but God created us this way. Our hearts and minds ask deep questions about who we are, why we are here, and how we should live, and we look to stories to provide the answers.

And yet, we aren't looking for just any story. We want a story that speaks to us personally. One that can unlock the problems we face or help us reach a new level of meaning and purpose in our lives. This is why the stories of the saints have always been so popular in the history of the Church. For Catholics, almost every day holds a feast to celebrate the life of a saint. Believers around the world read their biographies. At Mass, priests tell the stories of their lives.

Conversion stories of the saints are even more popular (St. Augustine's *Confessions* has been a bestseller for 1,600 years!). These holy men and women came from various backgrounds, but no matter what age they lived in or where they came from, their lives tell one very relatable narrative: the story of turning from sin, experiencing transformation, and seeking to do God's will.

The saints themselves loved these stories. As St. Ignatius went through his own conversion, he turned to the stories we remember about the lives of St. Dominic and St. Francis and said, "If they can do it, so can I." St. Ignatius was really on to something. Stories of transformation bring us hope. They give us the confidence that if someone else could pull this off, maybe, just maybe, God can do something in my life as well.

This is why storytellers are so crucial in our world today.

Archbishop Charles J. Chaput once said, "The 'truth' of our time in the world seems to be that there is no truth, that life has no point, and that asking the big questions is for suckers. . . . Thus the Church's task is to tell and retell the world its story, whether it claims to be interested or not."

I can't think of many people who can tell this story of God at work in our lives better than Tanner Kalina. A few years back, Tanner asked my wife and me to mentor him and his wife, Alli. We've had the pleasure of getting to know them as they begin married life. With my work at Hallow, I've also been able to see him write and produce episodes for Saints Alive. Whether Tanner is performing on stage, writing a new session for the Saints Alive podcast, or telling you about his day, he has a knack for storytelling. His stories draw you in quickly, bring you joy, and help you walk away with a deeper insight about God, life, and yourself.

There's something even deeper about Tanner's storytelling that makes it so effective. He is one of the most authentic people I know. St. Pope Paul VI proclaimed, "Modern man listens more willingly to witnesses than to teachers, and if he does listen to teachers, it is because they are witnesses" (*Evangelii Nuntiandi*, 41). Tanner's authentic witness sets him apart. It's what makes his stories so relatable and enjoyable. Just like St. Ignatius, we can look at his story and think: If Tanner can do it, then so can I!

In *Aching for Greatness*, he gives us a modern-day tale of conversion and self-discovery, one that we all need to hear. As he tells his story, Tanner reveals our own need to answer the deep questions of our lives. He gives a raw and honest look at the joys and difficulties of turning our lives over to God. Then, he shows us the tried-and-true habits that can bring about transformation no matter where we find ourselves in our relationship with God.

I could say much more, but you should just start reading the first chapter. If you're anything like me, you won't be able to put it down after that!

May God bless you and know of my prayers for you.

With Hope in the Divine Will,
Kevin Cotter
Head of Content, Hallow

# INTRODUCTION

# "NO SATISFACTION"

"Today . . . I consider myself . . . the luckiest man . . . on the face of the earth."

I stood at the base of my locker, dreaming about the day I would deliver my retirement speech. Cameras would be glued to my every move. Thousands of emotional fans would be on the edge of their seats as Lou Gehrig's famous words became my own. The whole stadium would be laughing and crying. Even the fans who had booed me for years would find themselves choking up as I gave one final curtain call.

My childhood dream was to become the next Derek Jeter—the next great shortstop for the New York Yankees. I longed for the day that I would dig into the batter's box at legendary Fenway Park amid the taunting of angry Boston Red Sox fans. From the time I could walk, baseball was the only thing I could envision doing with my life.

It wasn't a total pipe dream either. On this beautiful spring day, I was one step closer to my Big League, big-city dreams. I was a starting freshman on a Division 1 baseball team for Houston Baptist University (which is now Houston Christian University).

A lingering hamstring tweak had kept me out for the first part of the season, but I had fought through it and played in a handful of games up to this point. This game was different, though. On this day I felt 100 percent healthy for the first time in a long time, and I was playing against TCU (Texas Christian University)—the school I grew up watching and idolizing. I spent many spring nights as a kid dreaming about the day I would play on this field.

I took in a whiff of my tattered leather glove and admired the cap in my hands. The bill was bent exactly how I liked it. Echoes from the crowd and the stadium speakers trickled into the clubhouse, giving me chills. I threw the cap on my head, pounded my glove, and jogged out onto the field. Showtime.

My family and friends packed into TCU's sold-out stadium, the same stadium where I used to sit with them and, with architectural precision, construct a future baseball career in my mind. When my name was announced and my photo popped up on the Jumbotron in left field, a whole section of the crowd erupted in cheers. My best friend's "Let's go, T!" was easily distinguishable as it penetrated through the humid Fort Worth breeze.

Baseball meant everything to me at this point in my life. It informed my daily decisions—from the email names I created (yankeeman45@ hotmail.com) to the artwork I hung up in my bedroom, from the friends I spent time with to what I watched on television in my free time.

It was all I wanted to know about, and it was the only thing I wanted to be known for. When someone thought of me, I wanted them to think of me as a great baseball player. I wanted my tombstone to read, "Former major leaguer. Husband and father of three. Died from severe rheumatoid arthritis." I genuinely thought I was put on this earth to play baseball.

I'll admit my love for baseball was extreme—disordered, I might even say in hindsight—but I know we can all relate. We've all had, or maybe even still have, things to which we entrust our happiness. We've all coronated various pursuits as kings of our hearts. We are built for worship, and if it's not God we're worshipping, then it's something or someone else. We are never not worshipping.

As I walked up to lead off the game, I adjusted the straps of my batting gloves. I always liked them as tight as possible. A group of major league scouts huddled together behind home plate, scribbling away on their notepads. TCU's pitcher was one of the buzziest college names that spring for the MLB draft. I dug into the batter's box and stared him down. The pros were here to see him, perhaps, but they would leave excited that they saw me.

I laced the first pitch of the game to the right side of the field. The second baseman leaped up and made a dazzling play to catch it—an out in the books, but an impressive line drive to start things off. As I jogged back to the dugout, my fan base clapped and yelled to get my attention. I gave them a smile and a tip of my helmet before trotting down the dugout steps.

"Attaboy! If you keep swinging it like that, they'll fall," my coach barked. He patted me on the rear and stormed off. I threw a handful of sunflower seeds into my mouth and leaned against the guardrail of the dugout. The gorgeously manicured field sprawled out before me. The smell of hot dogs sweetened the air.

I had worked for this moment my entire life, but everything felt . . . the same. This game was no different than any of the others I had played in this season. The stadium was nicer than any stadium I had played in, and the noise was louder, but it felt like any other game. I thought I would feel a certain level of accomplishment as my friends watched me take the field. I thought time would stand still. I thought making it to this point would make me feel . . . known, in a way. But the game still had eight more innings to go, plus another two games throughout the weekend to finish the series. A confusing mixture of excitement and disappointment overtook me as the stadium lights emerged in the twilight. The Rolling Stones' "(I Can't Get No) Satisfaction" ironically blared as I took the field to play defense.

I ended up making not one, not two, but *three* errors that game. For context, most college shortstops don't make three errors in a month's worth of games. I was able to accomplish that feat in just one game.

I felt completely crushed. I felt like I had let down my family and friends. I felt like I had let down my younger self, like I had absolutely botched his dreams. I felt like my future was being pried from my clenched hands. Those professional scouts would never care to see me play again.

And yet, I also felt a weird sense of relief. For the first time in my life, my mind opened to the idea of living without this thing that I would have sworn I'd die without. I felt guilty for feeling this weird sense of relief, and so I tried to repress it with anger. It was a whirlwind. I think of Ron Burgundy's classic line in the movie *Anchorman*: "I'm in a glass case of emotion!"

I couldn't put words to it at the time, but it's clear looking back: that mixture of emotions was the realization that baseball would never satisfy me. It was a crushing realization and, at the same time, an exhilarating one. No matter how much success I achieved, there would always be more success to pull off. Even if I did make it to the major league, I would have to become an all-star. Even if I became an all-star, I would have to become MVP. Even if I became MVP, I would have to become the greatest baseball player to have ever played. And even then, I would have to live the rest of my life hoping my greatness stood the test of time.

I'm sure you, too, have placed all your bets on something or someone only to realize they fall short of satisfying. Or maybe you're banking on something or someone to fulfill you right now, and you haven't had this realization yet. But chances are good that you know that small, hollow feeling in the pit of your stomach that taunts you with the reality that winning or making the cut or getting the girl (or you name it) still won't be enough.

This is a great realization! In fact, I believe that we *must* come to this realization. We're all aching to be known—truly and deeply known. We're all aching for an infinitely deep intimacy, and we often look in the wrong places to find it.

The opening lines of the *Catechism of the Catholic Church*—the "hook" for all that the Church teaches—boldly declare, "God, infinitely perfect and blessed in himself, in a plan of sheer goodness freely created [us] to make [us] share in his own blessed life. For this reason, at every time and in every place, God draws close to [us]. He calls [us] to seek him, to know him, to love him with all [our] strength" (*CCC* 1).

"To make us share in his own blessed life." In other words, God created us for intimacy with him. He leads us into that blessed life by calling us to seek him, to know him, and to love him. The problem is that we often look for life outside of him. In trying to be all things baseball, I was ultimately trying to find life outside of God.

I fell victim to the age-old trick, the same lie that trapped Adam and Eve. As St. John Paul II once said, "The greatest deception, and the deepest source of unhappiness, is *the illusion of finding life by excluding God . . ."*

Of course, we will never admit that we try to find life without God. Only the staunchest of atheists will make the claim that God (or some higher being) isn't somehow tied to their happiness, and you likely don't fall into that category. So this is where it gets tricky.

Though many of us don't buy the illusion of finding life by excluding God, we do buy the illusion of finding life by *containing* God. In other words, many of us think that we can keep God at bay and remain the captain of our lives. We think we can navigate where we're going while we toss God the occasional bone. We want God in the picture, but we don't want him to *be* the picture. We pursue God with one foot in and one foot out. We know we need God, but we don't trust that he alone can actually satisfy us, so we look elsewhere to fill ourselves up. We say we worship God while we bow down before the thrones of success, pleasure, and power.

My friend, I've bought into this illusion for the majority of my life, and I still have to fight against it on a daily basis. I know it all too well, which is why I wrote this book. The aim of the following chapters is to show you how I decided to stop stiff-arming God. When I finally made the leap to actually follow him wholeheartedly, he set me on an adventure I could never have dreamed of. I hope you'll join me. He promises to do the same for you.

# ONE

# SOMETHING NEW

My baseball career's momentum puttered to a complete stop just a year after taking the field against TCU. Up until my incoming freshman class, my coaches only recruited junior college transfers. Not only was I the very first freshman in the school's program, but I was the very first freshman vying for a starting role. It was a culture shock to the upperclassmen, and they didn't take too well to the change. They were resilient in their bullying, ultimately confessing to me later on that they "tried to break" me.

And break me they did.

During practice, the first baseman would hold up his glove as a target for me to throw to from shortstop. He would remain completely still as the ball traveled from my hand to his glove, and if I didn't hit his exact target, he would let the ball whiz by. Even if I missed by just a few inches, he would taunt me and let the ball fly by. He would expect me to basically hit the bullseye from 120 feet out.

They engrained the idea into me that I had a throwing problem, which indeed *created* a throwing problem. I slowly developed "the yips," an almost mythical psychological condition that is made fun of more than it's understood.

If you're not familiar, the yips are a performance-anxiety condition. An athlete with the yips will forget how to do a basic physical movement that they've known how to do nearly their entire life. Golfers will forget how to swing their club. Catchers will forget how to throw the ball back to the pitcher. At shortstop, I forgot how to throw back to first base.

This only gave the upperclassmen more fodder to grill me with. My insecurities followed me wherever I went. Even if I walked into a party, they would yell "YIPS!" as a warm welcome. Their jokes even made some of my coaches laugh at times.

When you can't make a throw as a college shortstop, you quickly lose your peers' respect. You also lose your playing time.

I coped with the sadness of watching my dreams fade away by performing stand-up comedy at open mics. The trope of a tortured comic is a real one, unfortunately. Something beautiful happened when I performed, though. The mental weakness I felt on the field just so happened to be my strength on stage. The extreme shame that I felt over and over again on the baseball diamond gave me a certain level of fearlessness in front of crowds. I truly had nothing to lose because I had experienced much more embarrassing things. Also, my inability to stop overthinking when playing baseball was the flip side of my ability to remain sharp and witty when interacting with crowds.

Open mics slowly started turning into gigs, and eventually my Big League dreams started morphing into dreams of taking the stage on *Saturday Night Live*.

I transferred schools and changed my major to film. I was technically enrolled as a student at the University of Texas at Austin, but I took my classes at a local Austin improv club much more seriously.

Virtually every cast member on *Saturday Night Live* starts their career by performing improv comedy. It's just the first rung on the ladder one has to climb. *SNL* talent scouts scour improv troupes for the next big star.

I fell in love with improv during my time at UT. There's an old joke that America has really only contributed two things to the world: jazz and improv comedy. Improv comedy, or "improvisational comedy," is a form of live theater in which the plot, characters, and dialogue are all made up on the spot. Every single performance is a one-of-a-kind, never done before and never to be done again. It's one of the more remarkable things to witness when done well and maybe the most cringeworthy thing in the world when done poorly.

Entering into my junior year, I became the captain of the campus improv troupe. We named ourselves SNAFU (a WWII acronym for "Situation Normal: All F@#!ed Up"), and we would perform weekly shows on campus as well as around Austin.

I loved the freedom I felt when I performed improv, playing in worlds made up on the spot. I loved the high the audience's laughs would give me. I loved the diverse and eclectic nature of the people who gravitated toward improv. I even loved the smell of improv clubs. They were always in some rundown building, and whenever I walked in, a distinct aroma would immediately hit me—years of beer stains masked with egregious amounts of cleaning product. If you've ever been to an improv club, you know the smell I'm talking about.

And just like with baseball, the more I pursued my dreams, the more my dreams started becoming reality. I booked a role in *Everybody Wants Some!!*, a highly anticipated studio comedy, during my senior year, which cut my academic career short and shot me out to Los Angeles. Red-carpet premieres, late-night talk shows, magazines, parties in the Hills—it was happening.

*Everybody Wants Some!!* was the spiritual sequel to *Dazed and Confused*, the movie that helped launch Matthew McConaughey's career. The buzz going around was that *EWS* was going to do the same for a lot of the cast. (*EWS* is a college-party flick, and I'm not mentioning it to recommend you watch it. I'm embarrassed by decisions I made and portrayed in it—though because of that, I'm deeply impressed with how far God has carried me.)

Within days of landing out west, one of the biggest talent agents in Los Angeles invited me to have coffee at his office. The entertainment industry has a nickname for this particular office because of its influence around town: "The Death Star." In our meeting, he sat me down and nonchalantly mentioned some of the actors he represented—Melissa McCarthy, Jason Bateman, Miles Teller, and on and on. Then he looked at me and told me, "Tanner, in three years you're going to be on *Saturday Night Live*. In five years, you're going to be a regular in studio films. You're my guy. You're set."

I swaggered out of his office, slipped some cash to the valet, and sped off in my beat-up Ford Fusion feeling pretty good about myself.

Shortly after, I met up with my best friend in Las Vegas to hang out for the weekend. While we walked through a casino, a man came up to me. "Hey! You're that guy! Can I take a photo with you?!" He fumbled in his pocket and handed his phone to his wife before throwing his arm around me. I smiled for the picture before I had time to respond. "Thanks, man! You're hilarious! My friends are going to freak out!" he yelled as he ran off.

"Does that happen to you often?" my best friend asked.

"Of late, yeah . . ." I replied.

"Do you like it?"

"I . . . don't know."

Part of me *did* enjoy being recognized, but part of me also felt sad every time it happened. I thought being appreciated by the world would make me feel deeply known. I thought achieving a certain level of fame would make me feel comfortable in my own skin. But the only thing it made me feel was an increasing restlessness.

At this point in my life of faith, I still attended Sunday Mass. I would rattle off a few rote prayers before falling asleep at night if there was time. I kept a firm "no" stance on ~a few~ of the extracurricular activities my friends enjoyed. But that was really the extent of my relationship with the Lord. I loved God, but I loved acting more. I called myself Catholic, but I wasn't interested in doing more than the bare minimum the Church asked of me. I wanted to encourage others, but I wouldn't dare share my beliefs publicly.

And I wondered why I felt so antsy.

Just as I did in Austin, I dove headfirst into the improv scene in Los Angeles. I took as many different classes from as many different improv schools as I could. I loved it, and I also knew it would keep me on track for my *SNL* dreams. You could walk into any of the improv schools around town, and framed pictures of alumni-turned-*SNL*-stars adorned their walls.

During a class activity one day, it came out that I was Christian. The class froze. An acting partner said, "No way! Like you actually believe that stuff?" My class looked at me like I was insane.

I felt like I was admitting that I believed in Santa Claus. "Uh . . . yeah . . . yeah, I'm a Christian. . . ."

"Dude! I *never* would have guessed." The emphasis from my friend's *nnnnever* echoed throughout the classroom.

A cocktail of embarrassment and anger flooded my system. On one hand, I felt sheepish for being Christian, for believing in something so drastically different than what my improv-mates believed. On the other hand, I felt frustrated with myself for appearing so drastically different from what I believe, for not coming across as a Christian at all. It wasn't like my improv-mates were total strangers. We spent a *lot* of time together both inside and outside the classroom.

It was a harsh mixture of emotions. My stomach twisted into a knot. I didn't want to be known as "the Christian," but I also didn't want to appear so worldly that no one could recognize my beliefs in me. I wouldn't say this consciously, but I wanted to contain God and continue pursuing the life I wanted. I wanted to continue tiptoeing the line of following my beliefs and chasing the world like I had been able to in Texas.

But Los Angeles is a different beast from Texas. In Texas, you can keep God in the picture and remain the captain of your life. Los Angeles doesn't handle lukewarmness well. On the West Coast, you have to pick a path and run full steam ahead. In the months following that improv class, I felt a growing tension within myself. I knew that I had my feet in two worlds, and I was afraid to take the leap into one or the other.

When my agent told me to build my social media platform so casting directors would find me more attractive, I remember coming across a pro-life post that I liked and wanting to reshare it. *But what if my agent sees it?* I wondered. *He would totally drop me.*

When I found myself receiving VIP treatment at the esteemed Creative Artists Agency's famed Young Hollywood Party (the premier place to be seen), I remember feeling honored that people who had never seemed to care about me before were giving me attention all of a sudden. They wanted to party with me, and I didn't have the confidence to refuse. *Maybe if I compromise a little bit here, they'll want to be pals,* I thought.

When I struggled to find friends who shared similar beliefs and started spending more time with old castmates from previous film work, I remember feeling constantly left out for refusing to smoke marijuana. But it was how they bonded, so when my loneliness persisted, I finally caved to their offers. *Well at least I'm not doing other things I've seen people do around here*, I told myself.

After only a few months of being out in Los Angeles, I had pushed my faith down so often that I became numb to it. I stopped pursuing a community that could support my faith. The guilt I felt for the things I knew I shouldn't be doing started decreasing. I found it easier and easier to justify doing things contrary to my values. Not even intentionally, I was beginning to take the leap away from my faith.

And yet, I kept going to Mass. If I hadn't been to Confession, I opted not to receive our Lord in the Eucharist (which happened more times than not). Every time I went up in the Communion line to receive a blessing, something in me kicked over. I knew I wasn't living life the way it was meant to be lived. I knew I couldn't continue down this path. I was embarrassed by how quickly my heart could sway, and I felt increasingly timid in trusting it one way or the other.

It all came to a head one night when I was out with some new friends—one of whom was a cast member on *SNL*. As the party was winding down, we found ourselves on the balcony of a swanky home in the Hollywood Hills. Drinks in hand, the city lights spread below, my friend blurted out, "I'm so jealous you got to be in that film, man!"

"No way," I replied. "I'm so jealous of you! You're on *Saturday Night Live!*"

He looked down to the Hollywood lights. "No. Trust me, everyone in the cast would rather be in your shoes." His words stirred something deep within me. They confirmed the restlessness I was shoving aside. This guy had everything I was working toward, and yet he looked at me like I had everything he was working toward. We stood there in silence, both uncomfortable in our own shoes and slowly realizing that a pair from someone else wasn't going to fit well, either.

The questions grew crystal clear in my mind and heart: *Do I really believe this Catholic stuff or not? Do I take God at his word, or do I totally dismiss him?* Because if I did believe, if I did trust God's promises, then I knew my life had to radically change. No more hiding my beliefs. No more partying in the lifestyle I had fallen into. No more jeopardizing my morals for the sake of winning people over.

And if I *didn't* buy any of it, then the alternative was quickly losing its charm. Hollywood wasn't all it was cracked up to be. It was becoming clear that there was a carrot dangling in front of my face, and it would never leave. I could spend my life chasing dreams only to have bigger, brighter dreams slide in and take their place. The grass would always be greener on the other side. The twinkle of Tinseltown flickered behind the silhouettes of waving palms.

I was recognizing the black hole in my heart, and I realized it would devour anything and everything I gave it. It would never stop. *Saturday Night Live* wouldn't be enough. The next great studio comedy wouldn't be enough. An Oscar wouldn't be enough. Nothing would ever be enough.

Deep down, I knew that intimacy with God was the only thing I could place in that hole that wouldn't be devoured. I felt like I had tasted that wholeness once before and remembered a time when I was surrounded by friends who placed God at the center of their lives. As St. Augustine wrote in his *Confessions*, "You have made us for yourself, O Lord, and our hearts are restless until they rest in You."

I thought about giving God everything. I really did. I thought about it, and it sounded nice. But instead of running to God, I ran to the beach. Oftentimes, when we're met with a choice between two things, we invent a third!

I've always had an infatuation with surfing. As a little boy growing up in the middle of Dallas, Texas, I fooled my friends into thinking that I surfed and participated in competitions around the country. I spent a whole year in my elementary days wearing strictly Hawaiian shirts and puka-shell necklaces. In college, my best friend and I actually learned to surf over a couple of summers at a family friend's house in Baja California, Mexico.

When I moved to California, the very first thing I did after filling up my tank was purchase a surfboard. And then another. I surfed every day, sometimes multiple times a day if I could. I couldn't get enough of it.

Surfing is a sport of sensuality. It activates your senses unlike any other human activity. There's a reason so many surfers call the ocean their religion.

As I began to awaken to the idea that maybe, just maybe, my faith was the answer to all my heart's longing, I started surfing even more. I tried to ward off the shadows of God's call by making the ocean my church. Before long, there were only two things I wanted to do: surf and work—and the only reason I wanted to work was so I could surf some more.

The raw, intimate thrill of surfing led to a sense of intimacy that I longed for. I wanted to be fully submerged in something, and surfing quite literally allowed me to do that. It's an interesting feeling outdoor enthusiasts know all too well. I felt known by creation in a way. I also felt like I knew creation back. I had my special surf spots and knew all their ins and outs. I knew when and where the waves broke best. I knew when and where the other locals would show up. I felt connected to those other surfers I met. When I took friends to catch a surf, there always seemed to be a much deeper bond between us afterward.

Surfing gave me a level of satisfaction. This feeling wasn't sustainable, though. It came and went, just like waves do. It was here one day and completely gone the next, and the instability kept me coming back for more.

I tried to literally drown my unease in the ocean. The more I stuffed my anxieties down, though, the more they flooded me. Surfing is also a sport of silence, and the constant quiet on the water forced me to confront myself. I had to ask, *Is there anything that lasts? Do I really believe this Catholic stuff or not? Do I take God at his word, or do I totally dismiss it?*

One particular morning, I decided to really get away. I drove to a spot up the coast that I knew was fairly isolated. I just wanted to leave all these nagging thoughts behind.

When I had waxed my board and zipped up my wetsuit, I trotted out to the water. A gray marine layer caked the early morning sky. The tide rushed up against my ankles, bitingly cold. As the water inhaled back out to sea, my feet ached from going numb. I pulled out my long golden locks that had gotten zipped into my wetsuit and shuffled farther into the water.

I was the only person on the beach. I loved mornings like this—the waves all to myself, no wind, no sun. Only the ocean and me.

I laid my surfboard on the surface of the water and hopped on. Paddling out, I could see down to the ocean floor. It was a glassy, clean morning. Scattered rocks specked the seabed.

Past the break, I sat on my board and looked out to where the sky meets the sea. The waves rolling in blocked my view of the horizon line. They were bigger than I anticipated. They weren't monsters by any means, but they were definitely bigger than my usual spot near Venice Beach. When I caught my breath, I set my sights on a swell and began paddling. The wave spooked me as it caught me. I looked down at how steep of a drop-in it would be, and I bailed mid-pop-up. I gave a pseudo pop-up, one knee on the board and one foot up.

It was ugly. Anyone who knows surfing knows there's no such thing as a half pop-up. You either do it or you don't. You can stay low but you can't *not* pop up. The wave threw me off my board and proceeded to pummel down on top of me. Underwater, I must have looked like a rag doll falling down stairs. Somersaults, flips, distortions in every direction. As the water died down, I tried swimming to the surface. My hands reached out, but they grabbed only sand.

Another wave crashed above me and sent me spiraling and twisting in ways I didn't think my body was capable of. *Did my kneecap just touch my lower back?* Again, I tried scrambling to the surface to grab some air. And again, I grabbed nothing but sand.

By this point, my oxygen reserves were diminished—but the water doesn't care about that. Yet another wave crashed above me and sent me into Simone Biles mode. Spins, turns, snaps, the works. Ten out of ten. I knew that if I didn't make it to the surface this time, I was done for. I pulled the water frantically, kicked my legs as hard as I could, said a desperate mental prayer, and—burst out the water, taking a deep inhale of fresh air.

When I made it to shore, I unstrapped my surfboard and collapsed onto the sand. I lay there until I could catch my breath.

As my feet thawed, frustration started to replace my exhaustion. *Why did I bail? Why didn't I commit all the way? You either commit or go home!* As I beat myself up mentally, it finally dawned on me.

I was half-committing to the Lord. I was consistently bailing on my faith by never going all in. I would drudge through Mass on Sundays and then rage through clubs during the week. I would saunter into Confession and then turn right around and spring into the same sins I had just confessed. I would admit to friends that I was trying to treat my body as a temple and then I would immediately get high with them.

The ocean could take my life, sure, but the way I was living my life could take my soul. As I sat on the sand, the sun broke through the marine layer and glimmers of light bounced over the waters.

St. Catherine of Siena, the Italian mystic, once wrote, "Whoever loves himself or the world inordinately becomes incompatible with himself." I was tired of feeling like my own stumbling block. I had spent years arranging and rearranging things in my heart, never finding consistency or harmony. First it was baseball, then comedy, then surfing. You could sprinkle a few romantic relationships in there. Something or someone other than God always had control of my heart. Enough was enough. I had felt out of sorts for too long.

I knew that I needed to confront my faith head-on.

When I loaded my surfboard onto the top of my car and drove off, I wasn't the same man. The old Tanner died at the beach, washed away into the deep-blue waters of the Pacific. It was time to become something new.

# TWO

# GOING DEEPER

After recovering from my epic wipeout, I started to look for answers in the Bible.

A verse from the book of Revelation (3:16) judo-chopped me in the face: "So, because you are lukewarm, and neither hot nor cold, I will spew you out of my mouth." Other translations of that verse say that God will "spit" or even *vomit* the lukewarm out of his mouth. God would rather me be all *out* rather than half in? I guess it really *was* better to bail on a wave rather than haphazardly go for it.

It was time to seriously examine my faith. I decided to give myself up to Christ. Finally. Fully. There comes a point in each of our lives when we have to leap, when we're faced with actually pursuing Christ wholeheartedly or backing down from it all. We can't stand at the cliff's edge of that decision forever. I made the choice to jump—I made the commitment to really give Jesus a chance, to go all in and stop living two lives.

If you were to ask the hundred people I knew in Los Angeles what they thought of me at the time, you would get a hundred vastly different answers. I didn't want that anymore. I wanted to be the same person to everyone. No more masks. I wanted to simply be *me*. And so I handed Jesus everything. In the climbing world, they call this a *full send*. A climber will buckle down and stop at nothing to reach the top of his climb. Likewise, there was no more backing down for me. No stopping. Just completely "sending it."

I promised myself that I wouldn't back down from my beliefs. If someone asked me what I believed, then I decided I would share the fullness of what I believed. They could take it or leave it however they liked. I also promised myself that I would give *everything* over to God. This included my romantic relationship at that point, my friendships, how I chose to spend my time, even the artwork I made. Everything. Everything would flow to and through God. He would be number one.

If a firmer resolution to follow God would create friction with the people in my life every now and then, so be it. (It did.) If some of my friends stopped liking me because I wouldn't party in excess with them or joke about certain things, so be it. (They did.) If my managers and agent dropped me because I made "religious" content, so be it. (They did.)

I didn't set out to become perfect overnight, but I did set out to pursue holiness. Even though I still have a long way to go, it turns out that a simple, firm act of the will is a great start to that journey. Once I had accepted the fact that I would be different from a lot of the people I knew, I felt free to run full steam ahead.

My day job in Los Angeles was serving as a sommelier at a gourmet vegan pizza restaurant right next door to a magic crystal shop. (That is officially the most LA sentence anyone has ever written.) Needless to say, my coworkers came from ~very~ different ideological backgrounds. But as we cleaned up the shop every night, I would make myself ask them questions like, "What brings you purpose? What do you believe about God?" And then I would just listen to them. If they asked me to share, I would make myself share. I wasn't trying to force my faith down anyone's throats.

Almost every single time, though, my coworkers were genuinely curious to hear what I believed as well. So I shared, and I didn't hold back. And in doing this, I found myself growing more confident in my faith. Not only that, but I found myself growing more in love with my faith. They say the best way to learn is to teach. Sometimes the best way to catch fire is to share what little steam you have. Through the simple act of talking about my faith, my love for God further ignited.

But I still didn't quite know what to do with this growing flame. I knew how to turn away from the things that kept me back from God, and I was learning how to be resolute in my belief, but I didn't know how to move *closer* to him. I didn't know how to do the thing—to actually follow him and be in a relationship with him!

I didn't even know how to begin, but I knew I had to take a step forward. Any step. If I was going to follow Jesus, then I was going to *follow Jesus*.

Confession always seemed like a good place to be welcomed back, so I made a firm resolution to take Confession seriously. I wouldn't beat around the bush and only go when it was convenient. I would find a Confession time right away and get right with God immediately if I needed to. I knew I couldn't turn my life around in a full 180 without the confessional. I could probably give a 170 on my own, but if you march forward after only turning 170 degrees, you'll end up off target before long.

I also started studying what the Catholic Church taught in more depth. I picked up books written by the saints. I Googled questions about the faith that I had never received clarity on. I binged YouTube videos.

(Father Mike, thank you.) I devoured Catholic content like it was ice cream.

I also started leaning on my roommates, Christian guys who were also hungry for more. They quickly looped me into their men's group. Twelve of us men met formally on a weekly basis, and we also hung out whenever we could. We were committed to helping one another grow closer to Christ.

The house I lived in became the hub for the group—we called it the Glyndon because it was right off Glyndon Avenue. Guys walked in and out at their leisure. No one seemed to ever have a shirt on. The Glyndon's walls were decked with surfboards and bikes. Tobacco cans popped up in random corners and crevices. We hosted dinner every Sunday night for around thirty-five people in our backyard. It was just dudes being dudes—but how dudes *should* be.

The question *Do I take this seriously?* started to shift to *Do I know Jesus?* My concern transformed from *Am I a believer?* to *Am I a friend?* I grew confident that I was chasing Jesus, but I wasn't yet confident that I had a personal relationship with him. The guys around me talked about Jesus like they shared a friendship with him—they didn't just know *about* him, but they knew him personally and intimately. Their friendship with Jesus was attractive.

I felt a pull in my heart to go even more all in. I wanted that level of confidence with my faith. I wanted to be able to say without hesitation that I was listening to Jesus's voice in my life.

I made a dizzying discovery: once we step toward Jesus, a constant dare presents itself to take *another* step because Jesus constantly meets us with his presence and friendship. It's terrifying, I'm not going to lie, but it's also super fun. It feels like how I imagine a baby feels when they first learn to walk.

I accepted the challenge. I tried to commit even more to following Jesus, but again, I didn't know what else to do. All I knew was what a college friend once told me: "There is always deeper to go with God."

I knew Christians needed to pray, and not just a quick rote prayer before falling asleep. I knew that I constantly pushed aside the idea of praying for whatever activity seemed more entertaining or productive at the moment. Late-night Netflix: 418,973. Late-night prayers: 0.

The idea of doing nothing and praying was upsetting for an active go-getter like me, but I knew there was no following Jesus without it. Therefore, I started setting aside time to read scripture and pray every day. Reading scripture at least gave me something to do to pass that time.

Up until this point, I had never read scripture with any sort of regularity. If you've ever picked up the Bible, you know how intimidating it can be to simply start reading it. Where would I go? Genesis? Proverbs? Matthew? Romans? It was too overwhelming, so I started just reading the daily readings for Mass every day. Apparently, if you read the Church's daily readings every day for three years, you will read most of the Bible.

As I began acquainting myself with these quick daily reads, some of the stories grabbed my attention. I wanted to read them in their full context, so I would open my Bible to where they left off. Before long, the idea of reading through the New Testament seemed easy enough.

And as I read through the gospels, paying attention like I never had before, things started standing out to me. It was like those YouTube videos of color-blind people seeing color for the first time. The words popped off the page. Scripture blossomed in front of me. There seemed to be infinite layers to even the simplest passage! I found myself recognizing passages and references and themes between the Bible and Church teaching as well as our worship at Mass. It was like I had stepped into a vast web. "Wow! We say that at Mass every week!" "No way! There's the Eucharist right there!" "This ties into that, which ties into this over here! It's all connected!"

I found myself diving into scripture and loving it, but a deeper feeling began to pull on my heart. As I was encountering Jesus's presence in the Bible, I realized that all my energy and effort was not being matched with quiet and stillness. It was all action so far, and though the work was bearing fruit, I knew that friends don't spend all their time actively inquiring about each other—they also just hang out with each other and enjoy being in each other's presence.

I felt that interior dare to take another step: "Be still." But again, *where do I even begin?!* Is following Jesus just a succession of unknown ventures?? (Yes. Yes it is.)

After a while, I was encouraged by some friends to start praying a "holy hour." When I asked for clarification on what a holy hour is, they told me, "Oh, it's just an hour of prayer." Oh—"just" an hour? Well, OK then!

I was supremely intimidated, but I knew I had to give it a shot. If I continued putting off prayer for later in life, I knew I would never get around to it. So for my first holy hour, I went downstairs and picked out a chair from my dining room. I brought it back upstairs and plopped it down in my bedroom, right underneath the crucifix hanging over my door. "OK, I can do this." I sat down, closed my eyes, and took a deep breath.

After about a minute, my mind filled with racing thoughts. *I wonder how the waves are right now. Where did I get this crucifix—was it from my mom or my aunt? Why do some people pronounce* aunt *like "ant" and others like "awnt"? Who gets to make a word a word? Could* gridgelet *be a new word? It sure seems like* gridgelet *should be a word.*

I opened my eyes and popped out of my chair. I looked at the clock. *Five minutes? That was only five minutes?!* I started pacing. *I can't do this. I don't know what I'm doing. This is uncomfortable.* I looked like a caged lion during that first holy hour. I paced back and forth from the foot of my bed to my record player on the other side of the room. I felt accomplished when the hour ended, not only because I got my steps in for the day, but also because I stuck it out. I "prayed" for a whole hour. I, at the very least, gave God an hour of my time (which is all that prayer really is—a gift of our time!). I committed to praying another holy hour the next day. And the next. And the next.

After a week or so, I could sit still for ten minutes before having to pace around my room. After a few weeks, I could at least sit the entire time. Whether or not I was focused for much of that time was a completely different story. But after a few months, my life had changed forever. I couldn't pinpoint an exact day that it happened, but I knew that it had.

The more I prayed, the more I felt drawn to pray in front of the Blessed Sacrament. This made my holy hour sometimes more of a "holy hour and a half" because of the time it took to get to a nearby parish. However, I knew that sitting in front of Jesus changed me on a molecular level. Even though I couldn't necessarily feel things happening during that time with him, I saw the effects throughout my days.

I stopped leaving dirty dishes in the sink (a consistent source of conflict between me and my roommates). I felt my desires slowly changing. Talking about God with my roommates came more naturally and comfortably. My sailor's mouth became tame. Seeing former castmates from *Everybody Wants Some!!* in other movies no longer brought me jealousy but genuine delight. My need for success started to die. I grew stronger in being able to stop after a drink or two.

And I actually started to *enjoy* praying after a while. I even started *wanting* to go to daily Mass. My Sunday chore all of a sudden became my daily highlight. The saints—these people who had felt like far-off mystical figures for most of my life—started to feel less like superhumans and more like inspirational friends.

I was finally committing to a relationship with God. If I had spent most of my life with one foot in the pool and one foot out, both feet were now starting to get wet. I also discovered that I wasn't speaking into a void—God was speaking back to me.

In college, I would hear people pray things like "Jesus, I surrender myself to you," or "I give you everything." Those kinds of prayers always seemed flowery and extravagant to me. Whenever I tried to pray something similar, I would always feel a tinge of anxiety well up in me. I didn't really want God to have everything, but I knew that I *should want* him to have everything. But as I committed more and more to my relationship with God, I found myself praying for God to "have it all" and actually meaning it. I felt like I was in a free fall into whatever he wanted for me and wherever he wanted to take me.

I knew that the deeper sense of surrender I was enjoying was really God communicating with me. I believe he was telling me that I could trust him and that he was moving in my heart. I never heard an audible voice or had a profound aha moment, but I knew God was speaking. My world felt bigger when I daydreamed about a life lived for God. I felt a small spark of excitement when I thought about sainthood. I felt the strength to embrace doubts and distractions as they came, knowing they wouldn't deter me. And sometimes during prayer, a thought would pop into my mind—*I love you*—and would dance around my mind until it flooded me with a sense that I was on the right path.

I was beginning to taste the fruit of *finally* being bought in. I was beginning to grow confident that Jesus and I are indeed close friends. I didn't know it at the time, but in order to deepen my relationship with Christ, I was instinctively practicing the four habits that the early church practiced. These four habits are also what the Catholic Church asks followers of Christ to practice today.

These four habits are (1) learning and following the teaching of the apostles/Church, (2) fellowship, (3) the sacraments, and (4) prayer. They come from Acts 2:42, which describes how the early Christians followed Jesus after the Holy Spirit's descent upon the disciples at Pentecost: "And they devoted themselves to the apostles' teaching and fellowship, to the breaking of bread and the prayers."

This verse gives us the blueprint for intimacy with God, the roadmap to a restful heart. The third paragraph of the *Catechism* reiterates that all of us are called to practice these four habits: "All Christ's faithful are called to hand [the Good News] on from generation to generation, by professing the faith [the teachings], by living it in fraternal sharing [fellowship], and by celebrating it in liturgy [the sacraments] and prayer" (*CCC* 3).

If these four habits are what the early followers of Jesus did and what our Church encourages us to do today, then we need to practice them! We should see this as a signal—the Church is telling us, "Yo! Listen up! You want to truly know God? You want to satisfy that ache in your heart? Do these things!"

When I stumbled into these practices blindly, my life radically changed. Forever. Now when I practice these things intentionally, my life continues to transform. Every day. They are now as much a part of me as my own hands and feet. Even more so.

Our Catholic faith is an all-encompassing faith. Our Lord desires intimacy with us in every aspect of our lives. Acts 2:42 doesn't just give us four practices, it provides a holistic model for developing intimacy with Jesus:

The teaching of the apostles allows us to form *intellectual* intimacy with the Lord.

Fellowship allows us to form *social* intimacy with the Lord.

The sacraments allow us to form *physical* intimacy with the Lord.

And prayer allows us to form *emotional* intimacy with the Lord.

Practicing these together leads to a spiritual intimacy that satisfies our hearts' design. The harmony of these four holistic habits leads to what we are made for: holiness.

# THREE

# THE HEART OF IT ALL

The late-evening Pacific breeze caressed my face. I breathed it in, a refreshing concoction of salt and sunscreen. The golden glow of the sun inflamed the tired blue waters. The waves always seemed to calm down and catch their breath during this moment in the day.

Life was still hard. Work was still dreary. Acting auditions kept falling short. But I felt inspired. I felt like I wasn't fighting myself. I felt hungry for more.

As I sat on the sand and took in the sunset, I thought about all that the Lord had done for me in recent months. He was clearly moving in my life.

My heart was starting to feel more at home in my chest. I was starting to feel all the cliché things: peace, joy, love . . . y'know, the good stuff. I wasn't feeling them in super huge quantities, and they definitely weren't apparent all the time. But I was definitely feeling them more deeply. I somehow felt like these gifts I was receiving couldn't be touched, like they couldn't be totally removed from me now.

The past few months had also sparked a curious desire within me. I found myself thinking more and more about giving everything away and helping build the Church. I also felt insane!

I didn't know what that looked like, per se, but I knew that I wanted to lead others into this new life I was discovering and work for the Church in some regard. Now, following Jesus does not mean that someone has to have a Church job. That's definitely not the case. We *are* all called to help build up the Church, but that does not mean that we all should have a full-time position doing just that.

I still wanted to act. I loved acting. But I didn't *need* to act. There was a big difference in my outlook. And as each month passed, I felt an increasingly strong ache to serve the Lord in a more radical way than by simply remaining in the entertainment industry.

Was God calling me to the priesthood? Was he calling me to marry the girl I was dating? Or was he directing me to something else that I hadn't yet thought of?

The south skies morphed into purples and pinks, and my mind started wondering what in the world God was up to.

While in college, I had loosely entertained the idea of becoming a FOCUS missionary after graduation. FOCUS stands for "Fellowship of Catholic University Students," and the organization sends out missionaries to college campuses across the nation to evangelize students. College campuses have long been regarded as graveyards for the faith. FOCUS's mission is simply to reverse that trend and bring life back to young people during the crucial four years of life that we call college.

When it came time to interview with them during my senior year, I instead opted to attend a callback for *Everybody Wants Some!!* That film ultimately cast me in a starring role and grew to gain buzz, and any ideas of becoming a missionary quickly faded. A lot of my college friends did become FOCUS missionaries though, and the idea never quite left me. I once ditched FOCUS for acting, and here I was, ironically growing attracted to the idea of ditching acting for FOCUS—or at least something similar to FOCUS.

I stood up and wiped the sand off my legs. The beach gets cold once the sun goes down. The desire to share my faith grew and intensified—I had to do something about it. The idea of becoming a missionary dug into my skull. It became more and more exciting—more and more *terrifying*, but more and more like the adventure that was tugging on my heart.

I submitted an application, and suddenly, the ideas I had enjoyed juggling in my mind for months became real when I was called for an interview. In the conversation, I got the sense that I was indeed going to receive an opportunity to serve as a campus missionary. The weight of making such a big decision hit me. I knew that I would have to decide one way or another and *soon*. I also knew that my decision would change the course of my life forever.

I knew the Lord spoke to me in prayer, so I buckled in. If there was ever a time to pray, now was it. However, I didn't feel like I was getting any clarity from the Big Man. I made a list of positives and negatives for FOCUS and then a similar list for Los Angeles, but they came out pretty even. I mulled things over with my roommates, but they were excited for me either way. I didn't know what to do! Was I an absolute nutjob?!

On a run one morning, I told God that I would love a sign. Literally anything. Absolutely anything. I just wanted to make the decision that he wanted me to make. I immediately looked up and saw a billboard for the HBO show *Westworld*. "*Westworld* . . . *Westworld* . . . West! Does that mean that I should stay out west and not do FOCUS?" I shook my head. If I was looking for a sign, then I could find one in anything.

I ran to the beach to check out the red-algae bloom that had taken nearby waters by force. This red algae was all the rage because, at night, it would light up the water whenever it encountered friction. Waves would flash a beautiful light-blue color as they broke. The beach would look more like a nightclub than an actual beach.

The night before, my roommates and I had gone out for a midnight surf, and I felt like I was in an Avatar movie. As I caught waves, streaks of brilliant fluorescent-blue lit up behind me. When I paddled back out, my hands left strokes of light beside me. It was surreal. During the day, though, it was pretty plain. The water just looked slightly murkier than usual. I caught my breath, did some light stretching, then ran back home.

Later that night, my roommates and I trekked back to the beach to enjoy the water's light show. We couldn't get enough of it. As the waves crashed, blue light lit up the beach. We played with the sand, taking turns kicking it and watching the slashes of blue light that would follow. We were dumbfounded as we watched this strange natural phenomenon.

After a period of enjoyable silence, one of my roommates joked, "The only thing that would make this cooler was if that little dinghy out there were shooting off fireworks." Immediately and totally randomly, a single firework shot off and exploded in the night sky. I kid you not. There weren't any other fireworks that night before or after.

We all sat still, stunned by the timing of such a wild coincidence. Another one of my roommates turned to me and said, "Tanner, that means you have to do FOCUS." We hadn't discussed FOCUS the entire night. *What?!* It felt like too much of a sign from God to actually be a sign. My legs turned to Jell-O and went weak.

The next night, I cooked dinner for myself and grabbed a random beer from a variety six-pack I was given at work. A Mexican lager, my favorite. The TV was on, but I stared at the wall. I didn't want to make the wrong decision. It all felt so heavy. The more I thought about it, the more confused I became. The more confused I became, the less I trusted that I was hearing from God at all. As I finished my beer, I turned the can over. A quote read, "You are closer to him right now than most people will ever have the great fortune to be." *What?!* It was a totally random lager from a totally random six-pack. Again, it was just too obvious. I had to be making things up in my head!

Sure enough, FOCUS offered me a job a few days later. They only gave me twenty-four hours to make my decision. I asked for an extension, so they gave me forty-eight hours. Quite the extension. It was officially crunch time.

I decided to accept because the desire to serve God and his people was too strong to ignore. I said yes because I wanted to love God more and, in doing so, love other people more. God's love for us always demands a response. He takes us on an adventure unique to each of us, depending on our gifts and circumstances. Sometimes that adventure merely looks like picking up the phone to tell someone you're thinking of them. Sometimes it looks like going back to Sunday Mass. Sometimes it can mean becoming a FOCUS missionary. Sometimes it can mean doing something even *more* radical. It's different for each individual, but it's always a step toward deeper intimacy and commitment, which is beautiful.

FOCUS ended up stationing me at the University of Colorado, and I left LA for Boulder about a month later. Looking back, it feels trite to say that love changed my life. My story up to this point had been one of accepting God's love for me and then wanting to participate in his love for others. But somehow, describing the central driving force in my life as love feels empty in today's parlance. Love is in every song we hear on Spotify. When I think of love as the heart of my story, I immediately envision the Beatles belting out, "All you need is love," or rainbow posters saying, "Love is love," or hippies holding up peace signs saying, "Just love, maaan."

That sounds bleak, and the last thing I want to do is discredit or diminish love in any way. The core of our faith really is love, *but what does that actually mean?* How can I capture what was happening to me with a word so overused, undervalued, and ever-changing?

The word our generation needs to wrestle with today is this: *yada*.

*Yada*, pronounced "YAW-duh."

It's the Hebrew word meaning "to intimately know" or "to have relations with." A better interpretation is "to love covenantally."

*Yada* can also mean "to know" in the traditional sense. I can *yada* that the Civil War happened from 1861 to 1865 or that Derek Jeter's rookie season was 1995. Hebrew words are hard to nail down because one word can have a thousand different meanings. The covenantal sense of *yada*, however, is what makes this particular word stand out.

The best example of this type of yada, and the symbol referred to over and over again in scripture, is matrimonial love. In Genesis 4:1, scripture tells us, "Now Adam knew [*yada*] Eve his wife, and she conceived . . ."

A man knows his wife. He "yadas" her. He knows her in the most intimate way. He creates new life with her. This is what God was offering to me in this transformation I was experiencing. This is what God created us for! He wants to fortify us into his family. He wants us to share in his own blessed life. He wants us to bring that life to others! This is what it's all about.

Yada is everything. Understanding this little word in its fullness gives us the key to unlocking our lives. Yada is the current running underneath all of scripture. It's the motivation for the sacraments. It's the force driving all of our relationships. It's the force that drove me out of California.

Yada is the only way to explain why I made the decisions that I made, and it's the only way to satisfy the ache in my heart. We are made to know and be known on the deepest levels of intimacy, and that is what true yada offers us. Or, as St. Augustine of Hippo would say, the deepest desire of the human heart is to see another and to be seen by that other's loving look.

As C. S. Lewis notes in *Mere Christianity*, "It is when I turn to Christ, when I give up myself to His Personality, that I first begin to have a real personality of my own." When I belonged to Christ fully, then and only then could I truly be.

I was finally embracing covenantal intimacy—yada—with Jesus. I was orienting my life in a way that I could know Jesus more deeply, and I was waking up to the ways that he deeply knows me. This intimacy was bringing me such new life that I needed to share it with others, hence why I was drawn to become a FOCUS missionary.

Even though I left my career, my friends, the ocean, and so on—even though I felt stripped of everything—I felt closer to God than I ever had in my life. I was all alone, venturing into the unknown, but I knew that God knew me, and I knew that I knew God. Even though I was mourning the loss of my life in Los Angeles, I felt a greater love for life—for God, for myself, and for those around me.

I cried during my drive out to Colorado. I cried *hard.* Maybe the more accurate thing to say is that I *wept.* That transition was one of the most difficult periods of my life, and it didn't get easy overnight once I arrived in Boulder.

As I cruised down US Route 36, however, and the front range of the Rocky Mountains opened up to me for the first time, I knew that in that moment I was "closer to him than most people will ever have the great fortune to be." Tears rolled down my cheeks, but a sense of freedom flooded me. I was tasting the heart of it all. I felt the power of authentic yada—the ability to have nothing and everything at the same time. My life had been emptied—and because of that, my life had been completely filled.

We are created for intimacy with God. Yada is the design of our hearts. We get there through God's abundant grace and the four habits outlined in Acts 2:42, and once we get there, we have to bring others into it.

# FOUR

# THE TEACHING OF THE APOSTLES

My mom started working for the parish near our house when I was around five years old. She helped a wonderful religious sister named Sr. Ruth run the religious education program. Sr. Ruth was the person who first taught me about Jesus, and thanks to her loving efforts, I was baptized with my mom at the Easter Vigil just before my sixth birthday. Sister taught me four things: (1) Jesus is the best, (2) Jesus is really present in the Eucharist, (3) The saints loved Mother Mary, and (4) Dallas Jesuit was the only high school worth anything.

So when high school rolled around, I went to Dallas Jesuit College Prep. I didn't find out that I would be allowed to attend until a week before classes started.

Dallas Jesuit is an all-boys Catholic school situated in north Dallas right off two major freeways. It was a culture shock at first. I was surrounded by guys I didn't grow up with, there weren't any girls, we studied the Catholic faith in class, and we had to abide by a strict dress code. A family friend gave me all of his old Dolce & Gabbana suits, so I actually enjoyed that last change. I rolled up to class looking snaz-*zy*.

But I seriously struggled with those other changes. It was hard making friends right away. I liked girls (what can I say?), and I just didn't enjoy my theology class. I actually liked learning about the Catholic faith, but there was no learning that was happening in my class. My peers just wanted to goof off, and they'd tactfully steer my teacher (who was super smart!) into talking about Bigfoot or aliens or whatever random topic they felt like exploring. I felt discouraged being the only guy who seemed like he wanted to learn.

But during class one day, while my classmates tricked my teacher into discussing "energy balls," I looked up at the crucifix hanging over my teacher's desk. It was a typical PG-13 crucifix. You know how some crucifixes can just be absolutely gruesome? The kind that give you nightmares? Those are R-rated crucifixes. Then there are the crucifixes that show Jesus absolutely yoked with a small smirk on his face, as if he enjoyed getting nailed to a cross and humiliated by those whom he loved. Those are G-rated crucifixes. The one in my class was a solid PG-13 crucifix. It had some blood painted on it but not too much. It gave you the right idea.

I was moved by the love Jesus must have had for me. I was shocked that someone would go to such great lengths for me. I felt ashamed for the times I was disrespectful to my parents or a nuisance to my siblings. My mind started to wander: *Wow. Jesus did that for me . . . He gave his body up for me . . . I guess I have to . . . do that for him now.* I had a sense that love desired love in return, but I didn't know how to respond to what Jesus did on the Cross for us.

I started to feel anxious, and my mind continued wandering. *OK then! I'm going to become a saint. I'll just do it. No matter what, no matter the sacrifice. For better or for worse!* I made the decision right then and there that I was going to become a saint. (By the way, the decision to become a saint is never for worse.)

The problem is I had no idea how to actually become a saint. At this time, I thought saints were extraordinarily disciplined people with really extreme piety. I thought that we could will our way into becoming saints. After all, if sin was a choice, then why couldn't I just choose not to sin? I thought that I could do it all on my own.

I left that class feeling horrible. A sense of dread weighed down on me as I thought about what this choice would mean, "for better or worse." (The choice to become a saint should bring joy, by the way—just so we're clear.) I buttoned up my shirt, straightened my Versace tie, and tucked in my pants—a saint would never look sloppy, right?

Four years of absolute despair ensued. I became extremely scrupulous, extremely depressed, and extremely exhausted.

For four years, I didn't allow myself to look at my naked body in the mirror because I was afraid of vanity. Literally, I kept my head down anytime I would walk from the toilet to the shower.

For four years, I tried repressing any bad thought. This of course only made more bad thoughts race through my mind. It was the classic "don't think of a pink elephant" thing.

For four years, I would genuflect anytime I passed by a painting or statue of Jesus. Literally. That sounds crazy, but I thought it's what a saint would do. A saint loves Jesus beyond anything, so anything resembling Jesus should be venerated, right? It made sense in my head. (By the way, you're only supposed to genuflect in front of the Eucharist. Jesus alone is worthy of genuflection. We don't genuflect to material objects or other humans—just Jesus.) But I would genuflect to everything that had anything to do with Jesus.

It didn't help that my high school doubled as an art museum. There were pockets of hallways with Jesus paintings and sculptures lined up in a row. I'd kneel before each of them and cross myself as discreetly as I could, praying that no one would see me. Up, down, cross. Up, down, cross. I'd get a leg workout going from geometry class to physics. Needless to say, I started avoiding those hallways.

As you can imagine, my classmates caught on to my eccentric behavior, and it became even harder to make friends.

I thought I knew how I *should* follow Jesus, but it was leaving me absolutely exhausted. The problem was that I was doing this all on my own and in my head—I had no guardrails to contain my efforts, and I wasn't being drawn into communion with God or with others. I was white-knuckling it and trying to earn my way into heaven.

There's a reason the teaching of the apostles is the first habit mentioned in Acts 2:42. Romans 12:2 tells us to "be transformed by the renewal of your mind." We can't enter into a deeper, covenantal relationship if we aren't in tune with reality. The Church's teaching gives us just that: reality. It helps us see the world and our place in it as they really are!

In high school, I didn't know the fullness of what the Catholic Church taught. I followed my own perceptions of what it taught, and doing so led to my absolute turmoil. I wasn't in tune with reality because of that, and I felt it.

I felt crazy sometimes. I felt guilty *all* the time. But I ultimately felt *worn out*. I was experiencing the truth of that old saying, "Discipline without a relationship ends up in burnout." By the time graduation rolled around, I was ready to live life how *I* wanted.

When I got to college at Houston Baptist University, I was ready for a fresh start. I decided I would practice my faith when I could, but I wouldn't stress about it. I wanted to tap the brakes so I could make some friends.

But traces of my faith still lingered. I had a habit of making the Sign of the Cross before stepping into the batter's box. Since I can remember, I've loved watching Dominican baseball players make this action, so I implemented it into my game from an early age. It was honestly more for show than for any sort of religious practice.

During our first intrasquad my freshman year, my assistant coach saw me make the Sign of the Cross when I came up to bat. After practice, Coach Stockton pulled me aside. "Are you Catholic?"

"Yes, sir," I replied.

"Wonderful. There needs to be more of us. I'm going to make sure you're going to Mass every week, y'hear?"

"Yes, sir."

"I'm a coach, and I want you to be the best player you can be, but more than that, I want you to be the best Tanner you can be."

"Yes, sir."

Every Monday, sure to his promise, Coach Stockton would ask me, "Did you make it to Mass yesterday?" On road trips, he would find a Mass time that we could carve into our schedules somehow. Whether it was 7:00 a.m. or 7:00 p.m., even if we were in the middle of a doubleheader, no matter if it was blowing snow, sleet, or hail, he made sure we wouldn't miss it.

On top of that, he led a Bible study before Saturday intrasquad scrimmages. I didn't want to go to the first one, but he pulled me aside and asked me, "Tanner, you gon' go to my Bible study?" I really didn't have a choice.

I showed up, expecting my teammates to act like my high school classmates and turn the whole thing into a show. Instead, everyone sat stunned as Coach Stockton made connection after connection between the Old Testament and the New Testament. These two seemingly random halves of the Bible started to feel deeply intertwined. Everything was somehow beautifully connected.

Coach Stockton would also feed me CDs from Catholic speakers. I let them sit and gather dust in my truck's middle console until he started asking for them back. I knew he would ask for my thoughts, so I threw one of them into my CD player just so I could have *something* to say.

I threw in a talk from Dr. Scott Hahn. Why not? For an hour straight, I was enthralled. I kept driving around my block just so I could continue listening. It was thrilling to discover that the Old Testament and New Testament were intricately bound, that what the Catholic Church taught wasn't random and arbitrary. Dr. Hahn presented with so much clarity and research, there really was no arguing with him.

Building from Coach Stockton's efforts, I started digging into what the Church taught on my own. I made sure to attend any Bible study he led. I listened to more of his CDs.

Growing up, I always ~kind of~ knew what the Catholic Church taught, so I always ~kind of~ followed the faith. I mean, I grew up in the Bible Belt, and all of my best friends were Protestant. By means of survival, I had to have a somewhat decent answer for all of the big confusing questions they threw at me for being Catholic: "Why do you worship Mary?" "Why do you have to confess your sins to a man?" "Why isn't having just the Bible enough for you?"

But when I really started studying what the Church taught—when I began exploring the intellectual architecture of our tradition—I couldn't believe what I was learning.

Learning only made me want to learn more and more. I sought out answers to anything I didn't have full clarity on. The more I learned, the more convinced I became: There's not a single teaching in the Catholic Church that isn't geared toward yada—toward loving God more deeply and loving our neighbor more deeply. Every single *t* that is crossed and every single *i* that is dotted has yada as its aim. If you disagree with me, by all means please prove me wrong.

You don't have to become a master theologian to find freedom in the Lord. On the flip side of that, though, yada with God is incomplete if there's no trust in the institution that his Son founded in order to continue his work here on earth.

If you're like me, the word *institution* immediately makes you want to set a car on fire. But it's not just an "institution" that we're trusting when we follow the Church's teaching. We're not following a *what*. We're following a *who*. We're following the truths that the Holy Spirit has revealed to us. Following the Church's teaching is, at its heart, following the Holy Spirit. It's an act of the will to engage and follow what he has laid out for us. By trusting the Holy Spirit in the Church, we can grow to trust the Holy Spirit in the intimate details of our life. But you can't completely trust God in your life if you can't trust God in his Church. It gets messy.

When I was in Los Angeles, I felt conflicted about smoking marijuana. I suspected that getting high was probably not the holiest thing in the world, so I would try to smoke it lightly and avoid getting high. But even then, I suspected that I was playing with fire. So I did what many a person has done whenever they have a question about morality: I looked up what Fr. Mike Schmitz had to say about it.

I couldn't find a video from him directly around this topic, so I skimmed through the *Catechism*. Again, I couldn't find anything. I asked friends, but I received conflicting feedback. I scoured video after video and read article after article. The morality of marijuana wasn't like murder or adultery—there wasn't a definitive, concise teaching.

After gathering enough information, I found a consistent thread in all that I watched and read: the human body is a temple and deserves reverence. I knew this was calling me to quit, but I didn't want to. I was hoping someone would just agree with what I wanted. I told myself, *He said everyone is just trying to get high when they smoke, but I'm* not. *I'm just trying to take the edge off. What if it's a lower THC level? It could cause scandal, sure, but no one knows I'm doing it. You can't control how your body responds, but I know my body and I know how I've responded before.*

I tried justifying my desire to smoke in every way possible. Looking back, I'm baffled by how quickly I dismissed what I learned about the beliefs and principles that stood at the foundation of the Church's understanding of the human person and body. It was as if, once I was confronted with reality, I decided that I preferred my own ignorance just because it was easier.

When I let go of my own preference and opened myself up to wisdom from the Church's tradition, I realized that smoking marijuana only proved to be a stumbling block for me. It confused my emotions and headspace. It made me numb to my spiritual life because my prayer life slowly started to fade. My enthusiasm for the faith slowly started to fade. Only when I finally started to listen to the wisdom of our tradition was I able to find freedom. Only when I agreed that smoking didn't bring me closer to God did my mind grow clear enough to think straight. Ultimately, I concluded that someone should not smoke marijuana.

As people seeking to yada God, we shouldn't be content to tiptoe near the line of right and wrong. Our desire for intimacy with God propels us to live well above it. Our mindset shouldn't be one of "What can I get away with?" but instead, "How can I grow closer to the Lord? How can I reflect his goodness?" While I couldn't find a concise "do this" or "do that" from the Church when it came to marijuana, I was able to find enough to put the pieces together.

Church teaching gives us the guardrails to yada God—it provides light on the path to following Christ. As the great twentieth-century Catholic thinker and writer G. K. Chesterton once wrote, "The more I considered Christianity, the more I found that while it had established a rule and order, the chief aim of that order was to give room for good things to run wild." I saw marijuana as a good, or at least, I was told that it was a good by those around me, but I let it go in order to stretch toward an even greater good—one that I wouldn't have been able to see without wisdom from the Church.

In looking back, my stubbornness to not completely trust the Catholic Church only introduced pain into my life. Not trusting the Church made me, on a much deeper level, not trust the promptings of the Holy Spirit. I knew deep down that smoking marijuana wasn't good for me, but I pushed that conviction aside whenever it arose. I was too concerned with whether or not something was a sin when I should have been concerned about whether or not I was falling into yada with God.

Choosing not to smoke increased my trust in the Catholic Church. It helped me understand that I didn't have everything figured out, and if I was ever confused, then I could find guidance in a community and tradition much bigger than myself. The problem wasn't that I thought the Church was too small, but that I thought I was too big. I felt smaller when I gave up marijuana, but I also felt more *me*. I felt connected. I felt closer to the Lord.

The teaching of the Church can look like a long list of rights versus wrongs, but it's meant to be a field guide for intimacy. When I chose to shift how I viewed the teaching of the Church, I stopped feeling oppressed. I felt *free*. That's what yada promises us: freedom. No matter the situation, no matter the difficulty, we can be free.

OK, but wait wait wait. Doesn't the first habit from Acts 2:42 say, "the *apostles'* teaching"—not the "the *Church's* teaching"?

Aside from Christianity, no major religion's central figure claims to *be* God. No other major religion can make that claim. So right away, we have to confront that fact. We have to decide whether we believe Jesus—a real, historical man documented by numerous ancient sources—was a liar, lunatic, legend, or indeed the Lord.

And then within Christianity's 45,000 denominations, only one church claims to be instituted by Christ himself: the Roman Catholic Church. (Well, the Eastern Orthodox Church makes the same claim. Together, the Roman Catholic and Eastern Catholic Churches make up the two "lungs" of the Church, as St. John Paul II would say.) We have to then confront that fact. We have to decide whether we will follow what the early church followed, and what Christians have followed for centuries until finally splintering and dividing—or if we will set out on our own course.

The point is this: The Catholic Church has the fullness of truth and hands it on from Christ himself. The teaching that Jesus handed down to the apostles millennia ago is the same teaching that shapes our lives today. To return to our question, the teaching of the Catholic Church *is* the teaching of the apostles.

The more we follow the Church's teaching, the more we follow the lifestyle of Jesus, and that is what yada calls for. It calls for two to become one. It calls for the beloved to become so wrapped up in the lover that she becomes indistinguishable from him.

I grew up during the heyday of the WWJD movement. "What Would Jesus Do?" When Sr. Ruth gave me a WWJD bracelet, I wore that thing into smithereens. If we ever wonder what Jesus would do in our world today, we simply need to look at the Church's teaching. Jesus would do what the Church encourages us to do, because his Holy Spirit is the one informing all that the Church teaches.

This teaching is more than intellectual exercise. It is that, of course, but the truth is ultimately a Person and not a collection of correct ideas. When we follow the Church's teaching, we're not simply doing the right thing. We're configuring our lifestyle to the lifestyle of Christ. We're interacting with the Holy Spirit, who is just as active today as he was two thousand years ago. We're growing in yada.

When I learned about the Catholic faith in high school, I looked at the *Catechism* as an instruction manual, and I felt crushed by the weight of it. I found myself completely beat down by trying to follow what I thought lay inside of its pages.

When I started learning about the Catholic faith in college, I looked at the *Catechism* as an irrefutable textbook. I started to see that the Church's teaching wasn't arbitrary or random but in harmony with the totality of scripture. I admired it intellectually but kept it at a distance emotionally.

Now it's clear to me. The *Catechism* is a passionate love letter. It's kindling for an unquenchable fire. It was only when I allowed the fullness of the Catholic Church's teaching to penetrate my daily life by allowing it to conform my life to Jesus that I was able to find any sense of growing toward the yada God calls us to.

# FIVE

# THE WAY

During my time in Hollywood, I learned that there are two main schools of thought when it comes to acting: the Meisner Technique and the Method (Method acting).

I studied the Method, which is all about syncing an actor's inner life with their external movement. One can work "inside out" (basically feeling something and allowing that emotion to then affect your physicality) or "outside in" (allowing one's physicality to then affect your emotional life). Both are valid means to the same end, and every actor you watch works both inside out and outside in.

Method acting is rooted in sensory exercises. You close your eyes and relax. You then recollect a past memory, one that is particularly emotionally charged. As you keep your eyes closed, you recall what you saw, smelled, tasted, heard, and felt during that particular experience. By activating your sensory memory, you hopefully settle into a mindset or emotion that can then be taken into your scene work.

This is what Method acting actually is. The "method acting" that gets all the buzz in the media (the actors who never break character for

months and go to extreme lengths like sleeping inside of animal car-
casses or losing eighty pounds) is not the Method. That's publicity.

My acting coach in Los Angeles was known as a master of the Method. She's worked with basically anyone and everyone in Hollywood
at some point. Through her decades of training actors, her pulse on
human behavior is second to none. She deeply understands the human
psyche.

She enjoyed challenging me, and she pushed me to my limits in class
one night. She assigned me a scene that she saved for people who
were advancing through her program, so I was honored . . . and also
terrified. It was a heavy, emotional scene. The character assigned to me
had to break down and bare his broken heart. It was the type of scene
some actors drool over and some dread. I fell into the latter group.

I prepped and prepped the week leading up to this class. I did my
homework. On the night of my performance, I was feeling confident,
but for whatever reason I just couldn't "get there" when I was on
stage. The sense of grief and devastation that the scene called for just
wouldn't well up inside of me. None of my old tricks were working.
I felt hopeless.

With the stage lights burning down on me, I gave a very mediocre
performance. I could feel some of my peers squirming in their seats.
I felt like a crumby actor before my acting coach finally stepped in.

"Put it into your body!" she yelled. I haphazardly tried embodying
the physicality of someone who was experiencing intense levels of
heartbreak.

"No! Put it into your body!" I was too busy throwing myself a little
pity party to really go for it.

"NO! That's not what heartbreak looks like! *Put it into your body, Tanner! Commit to it!*" I finally committed to the physicality of someone

losing all he ever wanted. I grabbed handfuls of my hair, buckled at the waist, and punched the air. I let out a deep wail. I scrunched my face and began heaving. I went for it, and when I did, something crazy happened. As my body began crumbling over and shaking, the emotion inside of me sparked. My eyes grew misty. I couldn't tell if I was making myself shake or if the grief slowly welling inside of me was doing it all. "Good! Good! Now go! *Finish the scene!*"

Taking on the physical embodiment of grief filled my emotions with anguish and distress. What I did outwardly affected how I felt interiorly. The same thing happens with our faith—practicing the way of Jesus fills our spiritual lives with grace. Practicing what the Church teaches affects our spiritual lives. It's working outside in.

But then! The more our lives fill with grace, the more we desire to practice the teaching of the Church. It works from the inside out as well.

The Church's teaching gives us the chance to be receptive to transformational grace. Trying to yada God while discarding what the Church has to say is like trying to become a world-class musician without ever picking up an instrument. In order to yada God, we simply have to practice the way of Jesus.

And what exactly do I mean by *the way* of Jesus? The way of Jesus is what is revealed in scripture, it's what is taught in the *Catechism*, it's how the saints lived—it's the fullness of truth, goodness, and beauty!

When I wanted to be an actor, I didn't set out on my own to learn the nuances of performance and how to add complexity to my characters. I watched videos of masters at the craft. I learned from *them* as they broke down their process. I studied how Tom Hanks approached comedic roles versus dramatic ones, how Leonardo DiCaprio analyzed scripts. I studied how all the great actors got to where they are, taking note of the things they all did in common. I learned from the people who already knew how to have success, and in doing so I became a better actor myself.

The wealth of information and role models that the Church holds up for us is astounding. And it only increases over time as more and more saints come into the fold! There is wisdom in learning from those who knew God intimately and whose lives radically reflected yada. There is wisdom in following the path that has already been forged and not trying to forge one on our own.

Learning from the people who have already known the Lord deeply— the saints—positions *us* to deeply know the Lord. Why would I try to go about the spiritual life on my own when St. Thérèse of Lisieux has already shown me how? Why would I venture into my own views of sexuality when St. John Paul II, on behalf of the Church, has already unveiled human sexuality for me? How could I expect to change the world with my own values knowing that St. Francis Xavier helped convert more souls than anyone aside from St. Paul the apostle?

With over two thousand years of resources from the world's holiest souls, most brilliant minds, and most talented artists, we have more resources about Jesus than any generation before us. It's easier to yada God today than at any other moment in history.

To yada God means to know him intimately, to have a fully formed, well-rounded knowledge of him. If we return to the marital metaphor that appears in scripture so often, the more I know about my wife, Alli, the more room for intimacy I have with her. The reverse is true as well. The more intimacy Alli and I share together, the more I *want* to know her.

I want to know what kind of music she enjoys, the types of desserts she craves, how her family upbringing affected her both positively and negatively. The more in-love we grow, the more I desire to know her family and loved ones. I want to know what *they* have to say about her. I want to know all of her.

It's a beautiful spiral to fall into when done well. Maybe this is why Venerable Fulton Sheen described the Holy Trinity as just that: a "vortex of love."

We can get caught up in the same spiral with the Triune God. If I truly aspire to have a deep, personal relationship with him, then I want to know more about him. I want to know the scriptures that Jesus grew up memorizing. I want to know what the early church fathers taught about him. I want to know and honor his mother and foster father, the people he learned from and deeply cared about. Our devotion to Mary, in the words of St. Louis de Montfort, is a privileged way of "finding Jesus Christ perfectly, of loving him tenderly, of serving him faithfully." The more I know about God, the more my heart should desire him and the closer I should be to him.

At the end of the day, my acting coach was impressed with my performance, and she continued to invest in me. She even started allowing me to take her class for free (which was unheard of in Los Angeles) because she knew I was struggling financially. She was willing to sacrifice on her end to make sure I stayed in class.

The next class, she assigned me a scene right in my wheelhouse. It was a scene from a studio sitcom, and my character needed to perform some fairly elaborate physical comedy (my favorite).

I didn't do much prep throughout the week, because I had aced scenes like this a million times. They were my forte. All I really needed to do was make sure I had my lines memorized, but luckily, remembering lines comes easily to me, so I felt like I had this scene in my back pocket.

When it came time to perform, my class's lights burned down on me and my coach yelled, "Action!" I rolled into the scene with confidence. It was like clockwork, and I fed off my classmates' laughter. I could feel them enjoying it before—

"Stop! Stop! Stop!" My coach cut the scene short. "Tanner, what are you doing?"

"What do you mean? I'm doing the scene!"

"Oh yeah? Where is your character coming from?"

I stood silent.

"What's your objective in this scene?"

I looked to my scene partner.

"No, don't look at her. I asked *you*. What's your objective in this scene?!" She was starting to rise out of her seat like she did when she was really angry. "Where is your character going to next?"

I again stood silent.

"Get off the stage. Don't waste my time if you didn't do your work."

"But they were laugh—"

"Who cares if they were laughing? I don't care if they were laughing! People laugh at idiots all the time! I could tell you weren't actually *in* it. It was all fake! You phoned it in! Just because this is in your wheelhouse doesn't mean there's not more to get out of it."

"I'm sor—"

"No, I don't want your apology. I want you to be better. *Take a seat!*"

I sauntered off to my seat, embarrassed to make eye contact with my fellow classmates.

My teacher had invested in me, and I felt like I had taken advantage of her time. I felt horrible, but I learned my lesson. There are three things every actor has to know in a scene: where the character is coming from, what the character's objective is, and where the character is going next. Every actor you watch has these three things constantly running through their mind during a performance. A good director—like my acting coach—will stop an actor midscene and ask them one of those questions just to make sure they're "in it."

The Church's teaching gives us the answers to these questions. Every human in every civilization during every age has asked the same big questions. Why am I here? What's my purpose? What happens to me when I die?

Just as any good actor should be able to do, we should be able to pause our life and ask if we know the answer to those big questions. Are our answers informing the way we go about our lives? If we can't answer one of those questions, or if our answers aren't dictating our actions, then we're not "in it." We're not getting everything out of life that there is to get out of it.

Unfortunately, there is a lot of wisdom in the old adage "the longest journey is the distance from the head to the heart." It's really easy to know something and to have the right answers. To *believe* something, though, and to allow that belief to inform the way you live your life is a whole other obstacle.

And yet, Jesus *promises* us that ". . . you will know the truth, and the truth will make you free" (Jn 8:32). He also promises that he is "the way, and the truth, and the life" (Jn 14:6). In other words, Jesus promises us that knowing *him* is the way to freedom. It's not enough to simply know truth. We have to intimately know the One who *is* Truth.

The end goal of the teachings of the Church is intimacy. Relationship. Covenantal love. Knowing and being known. The teaching of the apostles, which flows from the teaching of Jesus, has always been and will always be geared toward yada. This is what it's all about.

And when we experience this yada, we transform. We're different than before. We become mini-Christs, lights to the world. Pope Francis teaches us that "the Christian identity card is joy." If we don't have joy in our hearts, then we are missing something. The mark of yada is joy, and following what the Catholic Church teaches should only bring about authentic joy.

# S I X

# FELLOWSHIP

Leaving college for Los Angeles, I knew that it would be a challenge to develop connections that were on par with my friendships in college. When I settled out west, though, it quickly dawned on me how difficult that challenge would be.

It only took a few minutes to realize that the handful of people I knew in LA did *not* care about the same things in life that I cared about. As soon as I dropped my bags down, I was basically offered a charcuterie board of drugs.

The friends I made on set and in improv classes were awesome dudes, maybe the funniest individuals on the planet, but Christianity was a foreign idea to them, an archaic concept or noble superstition at best. Even though we had different lenses by which we saw the world, I did what most anybody would do in that situation: I hung out with them because they were the few people I knew.

Their lifestyle was radically different when compared to my Catholic friends in college. Whereas my college pals liked to hang around a bottle of wine, my new LA friends liked to kick the night off with bong hits (and other extracurriculars). I was able to politely pass whenever they asked me to join them, but over the ensuing months it became increasingly difficult to remain an outsider. "Tanner, you're so good, dude," they'd say. Something about the way they always called me "good" made me feel bad.

Things I never had any interest in suddenly became huge temptations—simply because they were the norm for the people I was hanging around.

There's a popular adage that says, "You are the average of the five people you spend the most time with." I'm not sure how accurate that saying is, but it does echo wisdom from the book of Proverbs: "There are friends who bring ruin, but there are true friends more loyal than a brother" (18:24, NAB). We are communal beings. We influence one another. Iron sharpens iron, and just as well, iron dulls iron.

The second habit outlined in Acts 2:42 should encourage us to prioritize good friendships. In order to find intimacy with God, we need to find intimacy with one another. We need people who will sharpen us. We need *fellowship*.

One night, I went out with two of the few guys I knew. We decided to grab a drink at a brewpub across from the improv club we trained and performed at. From there, we would see where the night went.

We grabbed seats at a high-top, and I ordered my favorite IPA on tap. I didn't like IPAs in college, but after only a few months in Los Angeles I was an IPA guy. While we were cracking jokes, my buddy noticed a girl in a nearby booth with an uneaten burger. We waited to see if she was ever going to take a bite or if anyone was going to ever sit next to her. The burger just sat there and no one ever showed up.

One by one, we took turns walking up to her table and acting like a server: "Ma'am, is there anything else I can get you? If you're done here I can take that for you."

"How about another chardonnay? Are you done here?"

"Are you ready for your check? I'll get this out of your way."

It was a good bit. She laughed. We laughed. It was all in fun.

But after about thirty minutes, she came up to our table and dropped off the burger. "Turns out I wasn't all that hungry. Here you go, guys." Woo! We laughed and high-fived, and then she turned to me with tears in her eyes. The celebration immediately paused. Did we actually upset her?

She leaned in next to my ear and whispered, "While I was over there, I was praying, and I felt like God was telling me that he has big plans for you. Don't let those around you pull you down or keep you from him. He has big things in store. Keep going!" She stood back up and smiled at the group. "It's cooked medium-well just in case you like your burgers well done." And just like that, she was gone.

"What in the world was that?" my friend asked as he squirted some ketchup onto the burger.

"That . . . wow, yeah . . . she . . ." I fumbled for the words to explain. "It was just . . . meh, it was just a Christian thing."

"A Christian thing? Are you Christian?"

These were the people I was spending most of my time with, and they didn't even know I was a Christian.

". . . Yes."

Throughout the night, I couldn't tell if things were weird between the three of us or if I was just in my head. The jokes definitely died down, and there were a few awkward pauses. Surely I was just imagining things. But our plans for a big night on the town ended there at the bar. One of my buddies caught an Uber, and the other asked if I could give him a lift home.

In the car, my friend grilled me with questions. "So you're really Christian, huh? I guess that makes sense."

"Yep."

"So you don't watch porn or anything?"

"Nope."

"Do you think I'm bad because I do?"

"I think you're a good man, dude. I think porn is bad, but I don't think you're bad."

I never heard from my friend again after I dropped him off that night. We ran into each other a couple times at some parties, and we were goofy and cordial when that happened, but we never hung out again, and he never answered my texts inviting him to.

Lesson learned: If my faith was the thing that drew the line in the sand, then I would let it draw that line. Another lesson learned: My friends should probably know what I believe. Between these guys and my improv troupe, this was happening too often. I didn't like my faith feeling like a dirty secret that I had to keep from people. If I was keeping that part of myself from the people I called friends, then that's probably a telltale sign of the quality of friendship I had with them.

The Greek philosopher Aristotle taught that there were three different types of friendships.

The first type he considered was friendship of pleasure. These types of friendships are the ones in which both parties mutually derive some sort of pleasure from spending time with one another. The primary glue holding these friendships together is the fun shared between the two people. The friendships I had in Los Angeles were this type.

We shared the same interest in comedy, and we would go to shows together all across town. We enjoyed the same movies, and we would stay up until the wee hours of the morning watching them. We thought the same girls were cute, so we would take turns asking them out (and getting rejected). We had a lot of fun. But once something was introduced into our friendship that threatened the amount of fun we could have (such as my beliefs), that was that. We quickly drifted apart and went our separate ways. I still loved these guys, and I still do to this day, but our friendship was definitely rooted in the fun we had spending time together.

The second type of friendship Aristotle considered was that of utilitarianism. These types of friendships are the ones in which both parties mutually benefit from the other. Think classmates, teammates, coworkers, that waiter at the pizza joint you always go to.

In high school, my baseball team was super tight-knit. We'd go out to eat together before games, celebrate after, joke around in the locker room—we were a rowdy bunch. For some reason, yelling "CHILI!" was a thing whenever we saw one another in the hallway. We were close, but these were all friendships of utilitarianism. I helped them win, and they helped me win. I helped them become better athletes, and they helped me in return. Without baseball, I'm not sure we would have ever hung out. We were held together primarily by the benefit derived from our friendship.

While there's nothing wrong with these first two types of friendship, they tend to fluctuate as time goes on. Most of them come and go. They're rooted in the mutual benefit and enjoyment of the other person rather than the *good* of the other person, unlike the third type of friendship: virtuous friendships.

Virtuous friendships are rooted in something outside of the two friends. Whereas friendships of pleasure are rooted in the fun we have together, and friendships of utilitarianism are rooted in what we get from each other, virtuous friendships are rooted in a shared goal: the good life, a life of virtue.

These types of friendships are inherently deeper than the other two, and because of that, they are much more scarce. It took some digging on my part, but the Lord gave me a household of virtuous friendships in Los Angeles.

After a couple years of hanging out with random pockets of people here and there and grinding through different day jobs to stay afloat, my life came to a fork in the road. It was the classic red-pill, blue-pill decision. My living situation quickly fell apart, and my hand was forced. I had to find a place to live.

After a week or two of bumming it on friends' couches and living out of my car, I started to get a little worried. Would I need to move back home to Texas? Was I going to have to shell out an arm and a leg just to rent some dingy little studio in Glendale?

But then an opportunity fell into my lap. And then another opportunity appeared! When it rains it pours.

I could either live with a buddy from my acting class in an absolutely gorgeous mansion (no joke, a *mansion*) that was right off the beach next door to Don Cheadle (one of Hollywood's major superstars) and pay basically nothing for rent. It was this unreal, dreamlike scenario. I would literally have my own private waterfall and hot tub. I mean, c'mon. Who doesn't want their own private waterfall and hot tub?

Or.

I could live with five other guys in a small house (*small* is a generous word to use) right off Glyndon Avenue in Venice, share a bathroom, and pay way more than I would pay for the mansion. However. These five guys all talked about Jesus like they knew him. They didn't just talk *about* him—they spoke of him personally and intimately.

I was completely torn.

On the one hand, I could live the life everyone dreamed of. I could have financial freedom and the ability to do what I enjoyed most—relax by the water.

On the other hand, I could have support in my spiritual life, which was becoming increasingly rare in the frenzy of the West Coast. I could be held accountable for the way I was living my life.

By itself, it was a difficult decision. But the fact that I had a girlfriend made it an even more difficult decision—at least for me.

On the one hand, we could have the freedom to essentially do whatever we wanted, whenever we wanted. Even though we were striving for chastity in our relationship, I knew myself. My girlfriend was a much more disciplined person than I (praise God), but I knew that we would be isolated from the world, encamped amid some of the most beautiful scenery imaginable. No one would be lingering over us when we hung out. We would be in dangerous waters.

On the other hand, we could live life like I knew we should. Having so many guys constantly around us—along with my girlfriend's discipline (again, praise God)—would ensure healthy boundaries.

As much as I wanted to live in that beautiful mansion—man, was it beautiful—I felt drawn to live with those five guys. The way they lived life together was extremely attractive. They carried themselves with confidence. They were grounded. They even surfed a little—not a lot, but a little.

My girlfriend wanted what was best for me, and with her encouragement, I chose to live with those five guys, which radically changed my life. Forever.

Those five men encouraged me to dive into the Word, to pray consistently, to search out the truth and then live by that truth. They challenged me. They called me out when I fell short. They showed me that our Christian faith can affect our daily lives—that it should affect the way we live. And when it does, life can be joyful—life *should* be joyful!

Virtuous friendships are valuable. They're not easy to find, but we absolutely need to fight for them. Good, virtuous friendships changed my life. Bad friendships also changed my life, but for the worse.

So many of us find ourselves surrounded by plenty of friends, and yet when it comes to pursuing a good life, a life of virtue, so many of us feel terribly alone. Some of us have an abundance of friendships of utilitarianism and pleasure, but we lack any virtuous friendships. Others of us don't even know what it's like to be surrounded by friends of *any* type.

To yada God means to be a part of his family. Unless you're called to be a hermit, you need others who are striving to yada God to be a part of your life. Assess the types of friendships in your life. Don't be discouraged if you feel like you don't have any virtuous friendships.

But do pray for friends who can help you grow in virtue. Intentionally hunt for them. You might be surprised whom God places in your life. Take seriously the friendships you currently have and strive to be a virtuous friend yourself, who leads others to goodness. It took me a *looong* time to find the right friends, but I'm eternally grateful that I kept fighting for them.

# SEVEN

# COMMUNITY AND COMMUNION

My transition from Austin to Los Angeles was rough, and my transition from Los Angeles to Boulder was even rougher. Transitions are just generally rough, I suppose.

My decision to become a FOCUS missionary cost me a relationship, the career I had built, my community, the ocean—just about everything I held near and dear to my heart. With everything stripped away, I felt raw. It was an exciting time of growing closer to the Lord, but it was simultaneously a very difficult and trying time.

I questioned myself, but every day I chose to continue trusting the Lord. I felt foolish, but I also felt proud of myself. My heart was crushed, but it was also more alive than ever.

Boulder, Colorado, isn't dissimilar from Venice, California (which isn't dissimilar from Austin, Texas). They're all hippie towns. The air in these places is stained with marijuana and the sounds of street performers' guitars. They're surrounded by beautiful natural landscapes and vibrant personalities, and they each draw a fair amount of tourists. The similarity of the towns, though, made me feel even more homesick when I landed in Boulder. I felt like I was getting teased—like I was home but I wasn't allowed to actually go home.

Fr. Peter, the former pastor of the Catholic Center at the University of Colorado, saw that I was hurting and took me under his wing. Fr. Peter, or FP as he's known, is a former punk rocker, an avid kite flier, an off-roader, a woodworker, a jeweler, a poet, a mixologist. He's truly a man for all people.

FP and I hit it off immediately. His past as an aspiring artist gave us similar backgrounds and mindsets. Our multifarious interests gave us fodder to play with in conversation. Add in the fact that our backyards faced each other, and his rectory quickly became my home away from home.

One night, I brought over a bottle of wine that I had purchased in gratitude for the kindness he was showing me. I hadn't known him long, but I knew that he enjoyed Spanish wines, so I bought us a nice rioja. We popped it open and, as we slowly enjoyed it, he asked if I ever smoked a pipe. I enjoy cigars and tobacco on special occasions, so I told him yes. In a total FP move, he whipped out a Ziplock filled to the brim with special tobacco blends that he had hunted down in various places across Colorado.

We went out to his front porch and sat on his rocking chairs. His front porch overlooked "the Hill," where most parties—or at least the biggest parties—go down in Boulder.

FP opened a box and allowed me to select from his vast collection of pipes. He had short pipes, cob pipes, long multipiece pipes. I picked a normal-looking one, and then he showed me the proper way to pack it. You pack it softly at first, burn it to let it expand, and then use a pipe reamer to pack it tighter. "The proper technique allows it to continue burning instead of you constantly having to relight it. I've spent years perfecting this technique," he explained.

The rioja's spicy notes paired perfectly with the tobacco. As we sat on his porch and savored our juice 'n baccy, we talked about the origins of progressivism. We talked about the majesty of bristlecone pines, the oldest living organism in the world. We talked about the role of artists in society, and how we both feel a pull to play the role of an artist someway, somehow.

We also talked about movies. Fr. Peter is a film buff, which boded well with me being a former actor straight out of Hollywood. He told me that he could predict a film's entire story based solely off the first scene. After a couple hours, and after the wine had disappeared, we went inside so I could see if his claim had any validity.

Before we went down into his theater room, though, he introduced me to his best-kept secret: ice cream with peanut butter and chocolate drizzle. "People love ice cream, and people love peanut butter, but people never think to combine the two. This will change your life." After the first bite, he was right. My life was forever changed. My full bowl only lasted thirty seconds. His somehow only lasted twenty seconds.

Down in his theater room, I told him that I would need to play a movie that he hadn't seen in order to accurately test him. He told me to "choose away." I chose some obscure independent film that I knew he wouldn't have even heard of. As the opening credits rolled, he went deep. Like real deep. He started analyzing the colors on a character's desk. He started noting the changes in tone in the score. He compared and contrasted characters' wardrobes. And after the first scene, sure enough, he rattled off an accurate prediction for the rest of the film. My jaw hung open.

"Good filmmaking requires a story to be told constantly. Good directors know that. You know that."

"Huh? Yeah. No, yeah. No, I *totally* know that."

He let me choose another movie. Same result. With detailed precision, he predicted another movie's plot after only watching its first scene.

After proving to me his skill was no fluke, we decided to settle into a movie—something random that we both had never heard of. As the movie unfolded, the storyline grew eerily close to my own story. I think Fr. Peter picked up on that, so he would interject throughout the film with little nuggets of wisdom. His quips helped me see the film—and my life—through an ordered, Catholic lens. He helped me see the beauty in the characters and in my own experience. He helped me feel known.

The movie ended around one in the morning, well past both of our bedtimes. We didn't care, though. We'd had an awesome time hanging out. There weren't any truly profound things Fr. Peter said that night. In fact, a lot of what was said was just hot takes about the underpinning of the American government and why Spanish wine is secretly superior. It was profound, however, in the way that God can show himself through small things. Sometimes a good bottle of wine with a good friend, some pipe tobacco, and a flick is all the heart needs in order to know it's not alone. After all, God has been known to be found in wine, flames, and stories before.

My friendship with Fr. Peter was and is the most virtuous friendship I've ever experienced. He poured into me during my first year on mission (and since), which has only helped me grow more and more in love with Christ.

As C. S. Lewis once wisely noted, "Friends are like coals in a fire— together they glow, apart they grow cold." We are communal beings by design. We need one another, and when we are surrounded by quality friendships, beautiful things happen. When we are alone, it's much easier to burn out. This is simply the way we are designed. The Trinity is a communion of persons, and we are created in the image and likeness of that God. If God is Father and Son and Holy Spirit, then we are created in that image of community and communion.

Jesus gave two commandments to summarize his teachings: to love God, and to love others as we do ourselves (see Matthew 22:36–39). To be human is to simply be in intimate relationship with God and with one another. Part of the reason I was hurting so badly when I moved to Boulder was that I was being torn apart from the community that I loved. I was falling even more in love with God, however, because I was finding an even richer, even more intentional community. I didn't think that would be possible, but nights with Fr. Peter and the Buffalo Catholic community proved it to be true over and over again.

My friends in Los Angeles were all nondenominational Christians, but the people I was surrounded by in Boulder were all Catholic. I truly admired the faith I saw in my California pals. The Catholic community in Boulder that I found myself in, however, was simply able to speak my vocabulary and push me to greater depths.

But the fact remained that my transition was still extremely difficult. Often, our decision to seriously pursue discipleship with Jesus comes with some growing pains. This discomfort is a sign we are being stretched, which is good and totally normal!

But I didn't know how to handle these growing pains at the time. Fr. Peter was going above and beyond in helping me, but as amazing as he is, he's still only one person. One of the beautiful things about FOCUS is how deeply they invest in spiritual formation. They assign each missionary a mentor of sorts—a missionary with more experience to help navigate the ups and downs of life on mission.

The mentor they assigned me just so happened to be a friend from college named Sean, who went through a similar experience. The first time I called Sean, I filled him in about my life, and he patiently listened on the other end of the line. After our call, he proceeded to check in with me every few days. He motivated me when I felt like I had nothing left. He encouraged me when despair tempted me. He consoled me when I felt like I was grieving. He invested in my well-being. His random late-night calls just to ask me how I was doing meant the world to me at the time.

One day, Sean just so happened to be in Denver—a close-enough drive to Boulder. I drove down to the house where he was staying, and we made a day of it. We made carnitas. We drank some Shiner, as Texans do. And we simply enjoyed one another's company.

When his friends had gone to bed, we stayed up and talked. He opened up and shared more details about the heartbreak he felt when he left everything to pursue Christ. His decision to commit to the Lord happened around the same time that his engagement was called off. He told me, "Even though I felt sad—probably the saddest I've ever felt—I look back now, and that period of time was the most intimate season with Jesus I've ever experienced. You'll say the same thing one day, dude."

I wanted to give him a few . . . choice . . . words. Instead, I just nodded and let out a deep exhale.

"Trust me, Tanner. You'll look back and you'll see how rich this time is. Enjoy how close he is right now."

I didn't believe him in the moment. I just stared at the fireplace, the coals pulsating with red heat. But his words never left me. They gave me hope that the pain I was feeling could become a source of grace one day.

Sean's words have only proven more and more true as time goes on. Looking back now, I can wholeheartedly say that I've never experienced such an intimate time with the Lord. During that brief window of time, I *had* to rely on God—no one else—and I truly put my life in his hands. I was surrounded by people who pushed me into deeper and deeper reliance on him—no one else—and I experienced profound healing as a result.

If Sean hadn't told me that one simple line, I don't know where I would be today. If he hadn't planted that one tiny little seed of hope, it actually scares me to think about where I would be. *That's* the power of fellowship. So many people have grown closer to the Lord simply because a friend said something small in passing—they offered a small spark without even thinking about it. It might have been nothing big, but then it landed on a friend's heart like dry kindling and completely set it on fire.

St. Maximilian Kolbe once said, "God sends us friends to be our firm support in the whirlpool of struggle. In the company of friends, we will find strength to attain our sublime ideal." Real, authentic friendship pushes us into deeper yada with God. Real, authentic friendships are channels of God's love for us. They flow straight from his heart, and ideally, they scoop us up and run us right back to him.

I like working out. You might not be able to tell right away by looking at me, but hey, to each their own. When you're working out and trying to increase your strength to lift more, you have to push your muscle's capacity to the limit. You have to max out. You need a spotter to do this—someone to catch the weight if you fail and to assist you when you need a little extra push.

We can't advance in the spiritual life without spotters. We need friends to catch us when we fail and assist us as we progress. As St. John Paul II once said, "Man becomes the image of God not so much in the moment of solitude as in the moment of communion." Whether it was

Coach Stockton at HBU, Fr. Peter, or Sean, the Lord has consistently given me spotters to catch me when I'm struggling. Chances are that you have spotters in your life right now. They might not be the type of person you would naturally be drawn to. They might be the last person you could imagine yourself hanging out with. But if you don't give them a chance, then you might be missing out on developing strength in your spiritual life.

# EIGHT

# THE SACRAMENTS

When I was five, I had a blond long-haired cat named Fuzzy. I loved to snuggle with Fuzzy, but I also loved to lock him in a bathroom and touch his eyeballs and perform other experiments on him. Needless to say, he had some hesitations whenever I beckoned.

But for some reason, on this day, he came right up to me. He rubbed his side against my outstretched arms, his tail playfully swatting my face. I scooped him up and pulled back his lips so I could see his fangs. I touched his tongue to see if it felt like a human's. Not in the slightest. It was like sandpaper.

I buried his body underneath my torso and scratched his ears. As he began to purr, I remember thinking, *I wonder if he knows that he exists.* I knew that I was thinking thoughts, and I wondered if he could do the same. Isn't that weird that we can think about thinking? *I wonder if he's aware that he's aware—whoa. I wonder if he's aware that he's aware . . . that he's aware.* My mind spiraled out into a meta cacophony.

As humans, we are both bodies and souls. The animals are just bodies, and the angels are just souls. But we have both. We're like *angimals*. It's truly awesome to be human!

Because we are body-soul composites, we inhabit both a physical world (the world we see, smell, taste, touch, and hear) and a spiritual world (the world beyond what we can sense). The spiritual world is *even more real* than the physical world, but we lose sight of that.

Which is where the breaking of the bread comes into play in our examination of the four habits from Acts 2:42. The "breaking of the bread" is the way the early church referred to the Mass, the Eucharistic sacrifice. This sacrifice is the "source and summit of the Christian life" and one of the Seven Sacraments (*CCC* 1324). The sacraments unveil the spiritual world to us so we can grow in deeper and deeper intimacy with God. They are touchstones for the spiritual world through the stuff of the physical world. If you want to yada God, there's no better place to meet him than in the sacraments.

My bedroom door opened slightly, and my mom's face poked out from behind it. "Tanner, Nema and Papa are going to be here soon. It's time to get dressed." Fuzzy leapt out of my arms and scurried past my mom.

It was the day before Easter. I was excited to see what the Easter bunny was going to bring me. I mean, he brought me Fuzzy last year, so what could he possibly bring me this year? As excited as I was about the next morning, I was even more excited for that night: my mom and I were going to get *baptized.*

Sr. Ruth had worked with us both all year to make sure we understood the importance of this moment. We were about to become a part of God's family. We were about to become new creations.

My dad had to work, but my grandparents were driving up from Houston to celebrate with us. They only came to town for Christmas, so their presence only solidified my suspicions—tonight was a big night.

During the Easter Vigil Mass that night, my mom and I and other catechumens were gathered and ushered to the baptismal font. Monsignor met us there with a big smile on his face. His eyes shined underneath his big aviator glasses.

I was baptized first, then my mom. As the priest poured water over my head and baptized me, I didn't feel anything crazy happen. The water was a little cold as it trickled down my neck and dampened my white collar. The parish erupted in applause for me afterward, but then my mom went up and all eyes shifted to her. Was I really a new creation? Did all that much really change? It was over as fast as it started.

When I think of intimacy, I immediately think of the lovey-dovey feelings of a new romance or maybe the passionate gaze between two seasoned lovers soaking in each other's excitement. But this is a Hollywood version of intimacy.

If you were to ask an old married couple how they feel the most loved, they generally wouldn't describe the elaborate dates or lavish gifts from their spouse. They very likely wouldn't mention the fairytale vacations or even sexual encounters.

More times than not, they would say that intimacy arrives in moments when they found their laundry was folded for them or when their partner asked them about their day and really listened. They would speak about the moments when their needs were anticipated, when their innermost being felt seen and understood. That's what true intimacy is—when the deepest parts of who we are receive the selfless gaze of another person. There's a cheesy little saying that says, "Intimacy means 'into me see,'" but I think it holds merit. Intimacy is when someone sees into another.

That's what the sacraments do to us. They are moments when we allow God to reach down into the depths of our being and hold us. Even though we might not feel anything exteriorly, our cores become ignited with divine fire.

The sacraments are the everyday experiences of yada. They are the fountains where our longings to be known can be filled.

When I was baptized, my whole entire being transformed. The Lord welcomed me into his family. That's intimacy, even if I didn't feel much emotionally.

When I go to Reconciliation, my whole entire being gets cleansed. The Lord reaches in and wipes away all the gunk in my heart and restores me to right relationship with him and with my fellow humans. That's intimacy.

When I receive the Eucharist, my whole entire being merges with the whole entire being of Christ. I receive the Lord's body into my body. That's intimacy.

When I was confirmed, my whole entire being transformed yet again when I was sealed with the gift of the Holy Spirit. That, my friends, is intimacy.

I received Confirmation at the same parish where I was baptized, and it was scheduled during the spring of my sophomore year of high school. I had just been called up to the varsity baseball team for playoffs, which was a big deal. In Texas, playing on varsity at a big school as a sophomore is a badge of honor. Few people are privileged with that opportunity. Even fewer get to play on varsity as a freshman. That's reserved for the prodigies and freaks of nature.

On the day of my Confirmation, the second game of a big three-game series was scheduled for the early afternoon. With the timing of the Mass, I was going to cut it close making it to the field on time.

"We'll get your photo with the bishop and then we gotta go," my mom instructed me.

My godmother was my Confirmation sponsor. She held her hand on my shoulder as Bishop Farrell anointed my forehead with chrism oil and addressed me by the Confirmation name I had chosen: "Ignatius, be sealed with the gift of the Holy Spirit."

I mentally strained to fight off intrusive thoughts as the bishop laid hands on me. I didn't want to mess it up somehow by having my mind distracted. I knew that this was supposed to be a holy moment. The more I tried to repress my thoughts, though, the faster they came and louder they grew.

As I replied "Amen" to the bishop, my mind was spinning with horrible thoughts. Rather than feeling full of the Holy Spirit, I began to feel full of anxiety and concern. I fought to feel a semblance of peace or joy as the bishop echoed back to me, "Peace be with you."

"And with your spirit," I mumbled as I walked back to my pew. *Was I actually confirmed? Did I botch it? Did I need to redo it? If it actually happened, shouldn't I feel better?*

The irony of choosing St. Ignatius of Loyola as my Confirmation saint didn't hit me in the moment. I chose St. Ignatius because (1) I went to a Jesuit school, and he was the Jesuits' top dog, basically (he founded the Jesuits with five other men), and (2) he also struggled with scrupulosity, which was a big comfort to me at the time.

As soon as Mass finished, I sprinted to the bathroom and changed into my varsity uniform. My mom asked the bishop if I could sneak a quick photo, and then we busted out of there.

During the car ride to my high school's stadium, my mind kept wondering: *Am I any different? Did anything actually just happen? Is it OK*

*if I put on my baseball hat and all the oil wipes away? Would that undo*
*the sacrament?*

What I didn't know at the time is that God's speed is slow. If the sacraments performed like any other quick fix that our society has to offer, then they could be treated like those quick fixes—used and discarded. The sacraments are deeper and more profound than anything our society has to offer, however. The movements of our souls are a lot deeper and more profound than the movements of our emotions.

Even though I didn't feel anything peaceful during my Confirmation (in fact, I felt the exact *opposite* of peace), something profound still occurred deep within my being. That day has forever impacted my life, and I'm still experiencing the effects of it more than a decade later.

No one notices a forest fire right away. It usually starts as a small spark on a dry leaf or a cigarette butt on dead grass. But that small, unnoticeable flame then slowly grows into an all-encompassing ambush of fire that devours everything in its path. That's how the sacraments act in our lives if we allow them to.

The third habit of yada-like intimacy from Acts 2:42 is the breaking of the bread—the sacraments. When we practice the sacraments with regularity, we put ourselves in a position to know God more deeply.

When the priest says the prayer of consecration over the bread and wine at Mass and you receive the transubstantiated host, you encounter something completely different than the bread it appears to be: the Lord himself is there, beckoning you to deeper intimacy.

When the priest says the prayer of absolution in the confessional and you walk out, you leave completely different than when you walked in. It might not feel like it, but that doesn't mean something radically profound did not occur deep within you. The Lord wiped away everything blocking you from deeper intimacy with him and with your neighbor.

While I lived in Los Angeles, the Sacrament of Reconciliation changed my life. As I grew more and more weary of my duplicitous lifestyle, I made sure to find the nearest Confession whenever I knew I needed it (which was all the time). If that meant waking up early to make it to Confession before the workday, I'd be there. If that meant driving across town and forgoing my original plans, I'd make the drive.

There were so many times I'd be standing in the Confession line, kicking myself for being back again so soon. *Am I even sorry for my sin? Am I taking advantage of the sacrament? Will I ever be able to stop doing these things?*

I didn't want to be falling so often, but at the same time I wasn't strong enough to stop the lifestyle I had built. St. Paul's words from his letter to the Romans sum up how I felt: "I do not understand my own actions. For I do not do what I want, but I do the very thing I hate" (7:15).

Slowly but surely, though, the more I received the Sacrament of Reconciliation, the stronger I grew. I slowly started to gain the strength to say no to temptations I had given in to before. I could say no to another drink. I could say no to making that offensive joke. I could say no to lustful behaviors. The same thing happened with actions that I wanted to take on in my life: I could say yes to sitting in silence. I could say yes to admitting my beliefs when conversations called for it. I could say yes to reading scripture. My life developed a semblance of consistency.

Every time we receive a sacrament, something bigger and even more impactful than an atomic bomb goes off inside of us.

What is near these explosions of grace can no longer remain the same. The sinner is welcomed into the family of God through his or her Baptism. The sinner is freed from the slavery of sin through Reconciliation. Confirmation fully initiates candidates into the family of God and equips them to take on the mission of the Church. At Mass, bread and wine are transubstantiated into the Body, Blood, soul, and divinity of our Lord and Savior, Jesus Christ. Two people become one flesh through Matrimony. The priest is specially configured to Christ through the Sacrament of Holy Orders. The sick are healed of all spiritual infirmities (and sometimes physical ones too!) through the Anointing of the Sick. We simply no longer remain the same through the atomic explosions of grace that occur in the sacraments.

And when we allow the sacraments to work within us, the impact has a ripple effect that can expand and change the impression we leave on the world. The Lord's love intertwines with our hearts and radiates to those around us. One person, transformed by the sacraments, can shift the cultural landscape for generations. Frequenting the sacraments allows us to experience authentic yada with God that can—and *should*—slowly alter our lives as well as the lives of those around us.

# NINE

# THE BREAD
# OF LIFE

"When you tie a tie, you have to make sure that it has this little crease in the middle," my dad mumbled as he fastened my tie. "There we are. That's called *class*." He slid his knot up until it was tight around my neck and brushed my collar before taking a step back to admire his work. I looked at myself in the mirror. I looked like a seven-year-old James Bond.

I looked in the mirror and did my best Bond imitation: "Kalina— Tanner Kalina."

It was the day of my First Communion. Sr. Ruth had worked hard to make sure I was prepared for this day. Because my mom worked in the office with Sister, I spent even more time with her than the typical religious education student. She would let me hang out in her office and watch Catholic children's shows on her television, and she always had a pile of snacks and candy for me. Sometimes she would even sneak me unconsecrated Communion hosts to snack on. (Please don't hold that against her canonization process! She's a saint, I'm sure of it.)

Sr. Ruth also branded it into my mind that on this special day, the day of my first Holy Communion, the host I would be receiving would no longer be bread. It would have turned into the Body and Blood of Jesus Christ. I was blown away. Jesus must have been a massive man if his body could feed our entire parish! I was excited to see if I could taste a difference from the unconsecrated hosts I had eaten. Would he be chewier? Would he be sweeter? Would he taste like my favorite food? What was my favorite food? Cake? Would he taste like a slice of red velvet cake?

My stomach was full of butterflies as I walked up to receive Jesus. When the person in front of me walked forward to receive Communion, I bowed just like Sr. Ruth had taught me to do. I then took a step forward, held my hands high so Monsignor wouldn't have to stoop down to my level, received Jesus on "the altar of my hands," gently placed him in my mouth, made the Sign of the Cross, and walked back to my seat.

Hmm. Jesus still tasted like all those other hosts. I was confused, but I trusted that someway somehow his body was inside of mine. *How cool is this?!* I thought as I tried to remember the prayer Sr. Ruth had taught me to pray.

I squeezed my eyes shut and sat with my thoughts while the rest of the congregation received Communion. If I had truly just received Jesus's flesh into my own flesh, then this was a game changer. This meant the Creator of heaven and earth could dwell inside of me. It was a gift unlike any other gift. Speaking of gifts, this also meant there was going to be a big reception after Mass for the first communicants. Would cake be there? I hoped it would be the kind with thick frosting and not that light, fluffy kind. Maybe it would be red velvet!

My mind wandered away, but that first encounter with Jesus in the Eucharist stuck with me. As the years went on, my mom stopped working at the parish, and her weekly attendance at Mass slowly started to fizzle. There were Sundays when I would be left without a ride to Mass, but I would still skateboard to our parish, simply because I trusted that receiving the Eucharist was better than not receiving the Eucharist. I couldn't quite remember all that Sr. Ruth taught me about the Eucharist, but I trusted what she instilled in me: the Eucharist was no longer just bread after the priest consecrated it.

Growing up, I was drawn to the Eucharist. Even though I couldn't explain what the Catholic Church taught about the Blessed Sacrament or why, I knew that everything hinged around this core belief. If you took the Eucharist away, then the Church stood on sand. If the Eucharist wasn't of utmost importance, then absolutely nothing in the Church was important.

My best friend spent years trying to convince me to go to services with him at his nondenominational church. I would always decline because I simply trusted that having the Eucharist inside of your church was better than not having the Eucharist inside of your church. When high school rolled around and I became hyperscrupulous, my best friend's invitations to go to his church turned into long theological debates. He could always quote scripture, and I was always left fumbling my way through whatever I could regurgitate from my Jesuit theology classes. It wasn't until I attended the University of Texas that I could finally put words to my hunch.

My group of friends from UT were tight-knit. Virtually every night, we went over to someone's house and just hung out, and there were a lot of early-morning breakfast tacos and late-night margaritas scattered in between. Because I transferred to UT after calling it quits with base-ball, I gained the "freshman fifteen" pounds during my junior year. It was really more like the "junior thirty," if I'm being honest.

Along with movies, dating, music, and all the other typical center-pieces of conversation, the Catholic faith was a topic that my friends naturally brought up. We loved chatting about Church teaching and helping one another understand any misperceptions we may have had.

One night, we all gathered in my apartment and huddled around a few empty bottles of wine. My friend Gabe sat against my wall with his legs sprawled out in front of him. Gabe is a very tall man, so his legs took up half of my living room. "Yeah, I don't know. I want to believe it, but it seems too mythical, y'know?"

Jose, the definition of carefree, perked up. "I hear you, dude. Lord knows I've had my doubts. What exactly holds you up?"

"So we believe that the Eucharist is the Body, Blood, soul, and divinity of Jesus? That just seems too good to be true. If you were to walk into Mass, just a typical Sunday Mass, it doesn't really feel like many people actually believe that."

"Yeah, dang. Well that's our—"

I cut off Jose. "Wait, wait, wait. What do you mean 'soul and divinity' of Jesus?" I was trying to follow along with their argument in between sips of wine.

"Like, *all* of him is there," my friend Anthony interjected.

I looked around at my group of friends all nodding their heads. Rod snuck another bottle of wine from behind him and poured himself another glass. "Yessiree." They all knew something that I did not.

"Well, hold on. The Eucharist is his Body and Blood, but you guys are saying it's also his *soul*?"

"Yes!"

"Seriously? That's what we believe?"

"Yep," my friend Kaci chimed in. "You can't separate the body from the soul. So we believe that Jesus is just as much with us in the Eucharist as he was with St. Peter and Mother Mary when he walked the earth two thousand years ago. Rod, pass the wine. You have to share that with everyone."

Rod sheepishly handed Kaci the bottle of wine.

"Goodness. You're not even the one who brought this over."

I sat dumbfounded, rocking in my recliner and taking in this news. My friends continued their banter, but their voices were drowned out by my thoughts.

I grew up believing that the Eucharist was important. I held firmly to that belief. After all, the Eucharist was the one thing that kept me Catholic. I always knew the Eucharist was a miracle, that the bread at Mass turned into the Body and Blood of Jesus, but my friends were telling me that it was even *more* miraculous than I believed it to be. I already had awe and reverence for the Eucharist, but the Church taught that the Eucharist was *even more* glorious than I had originally thought. If what my friends were telling me was true, then we really did have the game changer of all game changers.

This same group of friends and I huddled into Gabe's van a few months later to drive to Nashville and attend a massive event called SEEK—an annual Catholic conference in which thousands of college students come together to grow deeper in their relationship with Jesus. We spent New Year's on Broadway Street in downtown Nashville before attending SEEK the next day.

At the conference, I was blown away by the number of priests who processed together at the beginning of Mass every day. It looked like we were all going to war. It was the most epic thing I'd ever seen. I was blown away that thousands of college students were all coming

together to celebrate their Catholic faith. It wasn't just me and my crazy
Longhorn pals chasing after it. I was blown away by the speakers and
their talks. One talk in particular broke my mind.

A few nights in, Fr. Mike Schmitz gave a talk about the sixth chapter
of John's gospel that opened up scripture for me like I had never heard.
*Wait, wait, wait. Jesus told the crowds* eight *times that his flesh was true
food? He doubled down when they were confused? He tripled down when
his disciples left him?? He quadrupled down with his apostles?!* I sat
in the front row, completely flabbergasted. Absolutely *flabbergasted.*
Listen, no one says "flabbergasted" casually. I want you to understand
how completely blown away I was.

After Fr. Mike's talk came adoration. Ten thousand college students
knelt on a hard concrete floor before Jesus in the Blessed Sacrament.
Sniffles reverberated sporadically across the room. *Are people crying?*
I thought to myself.

After an hour or so, a priest took the monstrance off the altar and
began carrying the Eucharist around the room. A monstrance, just in
case that term is new to you, is a big golden vessel that kind of looks
like the sun. It holds the Eucharist in the very center so people can
see Jesus. Monstrances are generally beautiful and ornate, and they're
designed to draw attention to the glory of the Eucharist, the True
Presence of the King of Kings.

As the priest slowly carried the Eucharist in this massive monstrance
around the room, he would stop in front of people at random and
allow them to take in the Presence of the Lord. You could hear people
burst out in tears whenever this happened. *Yep, people are crying.* I felt
weird about all of the emotion, so I decided I wouldn't be a crier if
Jesus came around my way. I was going to stay level-headed and not
let the environment influence me.

Well, Jesus came around my way and I was indeed a crier. The FOCUS missionary leading our group, Ben, was praying with me as Jesus approached us. As the priest walked, he stopped right in front of us and made the Sign of the Cross with the monstrance. I could hear Ben sniffling, and then I began sniffling, and then an immense amount of peace flooded me.

*This.*

This was why I remained Catholic despite feeling burned out in high school. This was what Sr. Ruth tried to teach me about when I was a little boy. This was the treasure of the Catholic Church.

I watched as the priest continued walking, holding the monstrance and Eucharist high. I understood why the Eucharist was the heart of it all, if even for a moment.

We are all walking monstrances in a way. We all hold something at the center of our life that we show off to the world. We structure everything around this center: our schedules, our dreams, what we read about, what we watch, the conversations we have, etc. For the longest time, that was baseball for me. I held baseball at the center of my life and structured everything around it. Then it was comedy. Then surfing. I've constantly adored other things in the sacred spot of my heart. And we all do this. If it's not Jesus in the Blessed Sacrament that we are forming our lives around, then it *is* something or someone else.

But only when we place the Eucharist there in the center where Jesus belongs do we start to find peace. Only when we structure everything around this gift—the greatest gift ever given—do things begin to fall into order in our lives.

I've shared about how hard my transition was in leaving Los Angeles for Boulder. But up to this point, I've skimmed over a big reason why it was so difficult. I was supposed to become a FOCUS missionary alongside someone else: my girlfriend of multiple years. As I discerned whether or not to become a missionary, my girlfriend and I had agreed to get engaged in the near future and move our lives together to wherever FOCUS sent me. We made the decision together.

But once I committed to serving with FOCUS, she called things off after careful discernment. I was heartbroken. I felt confused as to whether or not I should continue forward with becoming a missionary. I felt tempted to think that the Lord was punishing me for some reason. It was the loneliest I've ever felt, and I didn't have the motivation to do much.

But I leaned in. They say when the going gets tough, the tough get going. I say when the going gets tough, the tough lean on our Eucharistic Lord.

I prioritized daily Mass and daily adoration like never before. Even though it was all I could do just to get out of bed some days, I chose to trust that Jesus's presence in the Eucharist could put my shattered heart back together. Jesus heals, and I believed that Jesus was fully there in the Eucharist. Therefore, I chose to trust that the Eucharist would heal me. It was simple logic: a → b → c.

There were nights I couldn't sleep. Memories would flood my mind. The sting of heartbreak would overwhelm me. The endless stream of questions about what I might have done wrong taunted me. Doubts about whether or not I actually knew how to follow God's will poked at me as I lay in bed. Two very clear routes presented themselves to me: I could numb the pain or I could lean in.

In those moments, I would leave my house and walk to the chapel (fortunately, I had a key to the church). I would collapse in front of the tabernacle and just close my eyes. Sometimes I would lay prostrate. Sometimes I would just cry. But those late nights all alone with Jesus were some of the most beautiful and intimate experiences I've ever had. I felt completely known as I bore it all to him in the Blessed Sacrament.

Like the rising sun on the morning dew, the grace that pours out of the Eucharist burns away the impurities in our heart. It fortifies wounds and makes us whole.

Slowly but surely, this is what I experienced. Jesus did indeed piece me back together. Week to week, I couldn't tell the difference. Even month to month, my emotions fluctuated too much to notice any significant healing. But after a year, I was astonished at what the Lord had done in my heart. All the confusion, disappointment, and dejection had eased into understanding, hope, and gratitude.

That's a real miracle. That's a *crazy* miracle. When we think of miracles, it's easy to think about the blind regaining sight or the paralyzed walking. Those are really powerful miracles, don't get me wrong, and they still happen, but we often glance over the deeper miracles of the heart—the heartbroken finding forgiveness, the desperate finding strength, the rejected finding intimacy. These are even crazier miracles, but they're hidden, so we don't hear about them.

Jesus extends his veiled hand in the Eucharist to offer us these miracles (and sometimes even the physical ones as well). I've reached out and grabbed that hand. I've experienced this healing. If I could have one wish, I would wish that everyone would give Jesus in the Eucharist a real chance to do the same for themselves.

It's one thing to know the Eucharist is special. I mean, come on, the Eucharist is the *Blessed* Sacrament. It's another thing to understand the Church's teaching about the Eucharist and to have greater reverence for it. The Eucharist is the *source* and *summit* of the Catholic faith, after all. But it's a whole other thing in a whole other ballpark to orient your life around the Eucharist—to deeply trust in the slow purifying grace that comes forth from the Eucharist.

But this is what we're made for. Receiving the Eucharist at Mass is the most profound experience of yada that we can have on this side of heaven. This is the heartbeat of intimacy. And the Eucharistic sacrifice flows out into adoration, giving us the ability to spend time with our Lord whenever we want! We can allow the rays from his Eucharistic glow to penetrate our hearts and warm any coldness from the world. If you want to feel known, if you recognize your deep insatiable ache for intimacy, but you've never given the Eucharist a real shot, I would look no further. The Alpha and the Omega is here with us. Run to him.

# TEN

# THE PRAYERS

"Now I lay me down to sleep, I pray the Lord my soul to keep, should I die before I wake—" My eyes shot open.

". . . I pray the Lord my soul to . . . take." My heart began to pound. I tightened my blanket around me so no skin lay exposed. I could just . . . die? Before I woke up? Was this common?! It had to be common enough to be at the heart of a popular children's prayer.

I scanned my room, hyperalert for any possible sign of movement. The moonlight peeked through my blinds and allowed me just enough ability to see. My breathing quickened. The nightly prayer that I had prayed every night for years all of a sudden took on a different note.

A muffled clank outside of my room flooded my arms and legs with a warm sensation. My body froze, and I held my breath to be as silent as possible. *Was that the ice machine in the refrigerator, or was someone trying to break into my house?* I tried to stay as alert as possible until drowsiness finally overcame me.

The next night, I scripted a whole other prayer in my head. The old one had to go. "Please keep my family and friends safe, healthy, happy, close to each other, and close to you. Amen." I made the Sign of the Cross and felt a sense of relief as I drifted off to sleep.

I prayed this same prayer every night—or almost every night—for the next decade. "Please keep my family and friends safe, healthy, happy, close to each other, and close to you. Amen." It was my nightly routine. In the foggy moments before drifting asleep, I would quickly say this prayer in my head. If I had the energy, I would make the Sign of the Cross. More times than not, though, I would just cap it off with a half-conscious "Amen."

There has never been a more appropriate time to use the phrase "last but not least" than for the last-but-not-least habit of Acts 2:42: *prayer*. So far, we've talked about the teaching of the Church, fellowship, and the sacraments. In order to yada God, we need all of these, but we also need prayer. The other three habits come with their own difficulties to overcome, but in my opinion, prayer is the most difficult habit to practice.

In college, I befriended a FOCUS missionary, Ben, at UT's Catholic Center. Ben was a former LSU football player, so we had similar backgrounds in NCAA athletics. I was attracted to the way he carried himself. There was a spiritual authority about him that I had only experienced with priests. He was a totally normal dude, but he always seemed to walk into a room with confidence, humor, and holiness. At the time, I didn't really believe that those three traits could exist together, so seeing them all in another person made me want whatever he had.

Ben and I hung out here and there. He'd teach me how to change a tire or how to interact with the homeless. One time, he challenged me to walk around UT's campus with him and ask random people what they thought about Jesus. I didn't enjoy that walk too much, but at the same time, I admired how easily and unaggressively he was able to talk to strangers about their beliefs.

He was a great role model, and he earned my respect. Every single time we hung out, however, he would ask me, "How's your prayer life?"

Every single time. He asked me to the point that I stopped hanging out with him. I didn't know how to answer that question. I felt like I never had anything new to say. I (maybe) tried some of the approaches he taught me a couple times, but for the most part my prayer life consisted of that same little prayer before bedtime that I had memorized—and that was about it.

I ran from Ben's question, but those four words became seared into my mind: "How's your prayer life?" Anytime I walked by a Catholic church: "How's your prayer life?" Anytime I was doing something I knew I shouldn't be doing: "How's your prayer life?" Anytime I found myself bored and unsure of what to do with myself: "How's your prayer life?"

His question haunted me and followed me out to Los Angeles. When I finally decided to address it, I realized it was really asking deeper questions: *Did I believe there was more to experience in life? If so, was I giving myself a chance to experience it?*

I knew that there had to be more to prayer. I also knew, therefore, that there had to be more to life. Even though I stayed loyal to saying my little prayer before bedtime, I knew I wasn't giving myself a chance to experience more. I let chunks of time pass by me every day in which I could have stopped to pray.

One night in Los Angeles, I had a hard time falling asleep. I mustered the energy to make the Sign of the Cross and then rolled off my deeply rehearsed line: "Please keep my family and friends safe, healthy, happy, close to each other, and close to you. Amen." As I lay awake, I thought about what else I could pray for. Were there any tragedies happening around the world that I could pray for? Did any of my friends have something going on that they could use an extra prayer for? Was this all prayer was?

A passing car's headlights swept across my room's ceiling. A helicopter buzzed outside of my bedroom window. Or was there something more to it? Was I doing it . . . correctly? Was I doing it at all? I felt completely numb saying my usual prayer. Surely I was missing something?

I had no clue what I was doing, so I simply said, "Lord, I don't know what to say, but I love you. Amen." I chose to keep saying something along those lines night after night. I didn't know it at the time, but that decision was actually profoundly prayerful.

Quoting Romans 8:26, the *Catechism* explains that "only when we humbly acknowledge that 'we do not know how to pray as we ought,' are we ready to receive freely the gift of prayer" (2559). The first step to praying, according to the Church's teaching, is to admit that we don't know how to pray! That's a wild teaching (and also proof that the Church's teaching is acutely wise). I didn't know what I was doing back then, and I still don't today. And that's OK! None of us do.

My humble little prayer before bedtime gradually became riskier, more personal. I found myself praying for specific intentions—for my siblings' health, for my coworkers' conversion, for greater trust in the Lord. I also found myself thanking God for various blessings in my life—for my health, for the ability to set aside a little bit of money, for a pleasant conversation I had with a friend that day.

After a while, I found myself wanting to give prayer a real shot. I didn't want it to remain a stargazed soliloquy before bedtime. I wanted it to be something that I legitimately made time for.

I quickly learned that it's scary to begin praying. I didn't want to do it wrong (as if that's something I could actually do)! But I forced myself to eventually go for it. Just like in dating, you can't mosey around. You eventually have to go on a first date to get to know someone. You have to put yourself out there. The same is true with the Lord. He's waiting, and he'll never say no when we reach out. We just have to put ourselves out there.

I had no clue what to do, and I felt intimidated by the endless routes that my prayer could take, so I started with simply reading the daily readings of the Church. That eventually morphed into reading scripture and other spiritual books. Some days, I would just open the Bible or a spiritual book and read until I felt like I should pause and let something soak in. Some days, I would just go on long, quiet walks and talk to God about whatever was on my mind. Sometimes I would throw a Rosary in during those walks. Some days, my prayer looked like a combination of all of the above.

The Catholic Church also teaches us in the *Catechism* that "there are as many paths of prayer as there are persons who pray" (2672). Prayer is totally unique to each individual person. So not only do you not have to know what you're doing, but your prayer doesn't have to look a certain way. You don't have to pray exactly how I pray and vice versa.

We are each completely unique and unrepeatable, and so the Lord speaks to each of us in unique and unrepeatable ways. I have a friend I consider to be a holy dude, who is convinced that the Lord speaks to him through his Spotify. As he listens to music, certain lyrics will pop out at him, and he'll encounter the Lord within those. That's a part of his prayer life. That is not how the Lord speaks to me at all, and that is totally OK. I think the Lord knows that I am more likely to break out playing air guitar than I am to break out in praise.

I've mentioned that when I started pursuing prayer more intentionally, I eventually felt a pull to be silent. I've heard it explained to me that praying is talking to God and silence is listening to God. Any intimate relationship needs both to thrive.

And when I first tried sitting in silence, I didn't know how to sit still. My mind wandered. There were days I would spend more time wondering about random facts than I would thinking about God's presence. (For example, how aren't we all bald? We apparently shed anywhere between fifty to one hundred hairs per day. Wouldn't that eventually mean every hair has been shed? And I get that hairs grow back, but in that case why isn't our hair just constantly short or uneven? It's a mystery!)

But the more I practiced sitting in silence, the easier it became to rein my attention back in. It's never become *easy,* but it has become *easier.*

The more accustomed I became to sitting in silence, the more comfortable I became with vulnerability when I actually did choose to speak to God. When I talked to God, it didn't have to be all petitions or nice, fluffy thoughts. I trusted that it could be messy.

The first prayer in the Bible—or the first *spoken* prayer in the Bible, I should say—comes from Abraham in Genesis 15. In that prayer, Abraham complains to God. The first spoken prayer in the Bible is a complaint! I find that hilarious and also very freeing. I can talk to God just like I talk to my brother or best friend. I can let him know what's really on my mind and where I'm struggling. I can let him know that I'm disappointed and that I'm tempted to feel frustration with him or even despair.

That's what prayer is. It's a person being real with another person. You can't feel seen if you don't let the other see all of you. God wants to see *all* of us, because he wants to show us all of himself. And sometimes the Lord will stir uncomfortable things within us so we can talk about them to him.

When I was mid-heartbreak, memories of my relationship would flash in my mind like a highlight reel on YouTube. I would try to shove these mental images down and continue focusing on nice things, but then they would rush back all the more. It didn't take me long to realize that

God was stirring those things up to heal them. What isn't transformed gets transmitted, so they say.

When these images bombarded my prayer, I let God have an earful. I let him know that I was disappointed. I let him know that I didn't understand what he was doing. I let him know that it was hard to trust him. I let him know that it was hard to trust *myself*, because my prayer was revealing to me all the ways I could have been more selfless and loving. I let him have it all. However, I also told him that I would continue trusting him—even though sometimes I didn't want to. I told him that I knew he was doing something for my good—even if it didn't feel like it at the time.

Constantly showing up and ruthlessly trusting God allowed God to work. He took my heartbreak and allowed me to see the deeper ache within my heart. He allowed me to expose all my emotions to him so that he could reveal me to myself.

I thought I had finally met someone (my previous girlfriend) who was willing to see me and deeply know me. When we went our separate ways, I was left with a gaping hole in my heart, completely vulnerable and hurt. God used that pain to point me to the fact that no person would ever be able to truly see me, as I am at my core. The very deepest depths of my being were unknowable and reserved for God alone. Even though I was indeed aching for the loss of a wonderful woman and good friend, I was really aching for something only God could give me. All along, it was God's love that I had been longing for, but I was looking for someone else to make me whole—an impossible task.

Instead of covering that gaping hole in my heart with more pursuits or more numbing agents, I continuously exposed it to God in prayer, and he continuously poured himself into it in return. When I accepted that the deeper ache in my heart was really for God, he rushed in like a wild tide. The levee broke. As Venerable Fulton Sheen once said,

"Sometimes the only way the good Lord can get into some hearts is to break them."

The Lord wants all of us. That's what the fullness of intimacy craves. Not just the good parts. Not just the roses. *All* of it. Like a passionate lover, he will stand at the door of our hearts and knock until we let him in.

Prayer opens the door to let God in. Not only that, but prayer breaks down the levees we build in our hearts that keep him contained. God is too wild to contain. He's too powerful to flow in one defined direction. He wants to break free in our lives and seep into our pores. He wants to flood us with himself. Prayer is how we allow that to happen.

When I first began exploring my prayer life, I would say that my prayer was solid. I prioritized it every day. Nothing would stop me from carving out time each day to spend with the Lord. I felt like the Lord really spoke to me and consoled me through hard times. I felt his presence during my moments of silence. I actually grew to really enjoy my times of prayer.

In the years following that initial period, I have continued prioritizing my prayer life. It's ingrained into my day-to-day schedule. However, there are periods when it feels really dry and the Lord's voice is extremely hard to hear. There are periods when I'm really tired and it's almost impossible to concentrate. There are periods when I simply don't feel like praying—but I continue to show up regardless. And because of that, because I continue to show up, I would say that my prayer life is even more solid than it was when it felt so vibrant. Even though I feel the Lord's proximity less often, I would say that I'm even closer to the Lord than when I once felt his presence so strongly and consistently. I would also say that I still have no idea what I'm doing, but I will continue showing up each day to give it my best shot.

In the past, if I prayed and walked away feeling like I didn't get anything out of it, I would leave discouraged or anxious. I would maybe even beat myself up: *I should have focused harder! I can't hear God! He's not speaking to me!*

But now, if I feel like I didn't get anything out of my time in prayer, I'm grateful that I was able to spend some time in God's presence at the very least. It's kind of like dating. In the beginning stages of dating someone, leaving a date not knowing how the other person feels about you can be really discouraging or anxiety-provoking. *I should have made it more fun! They might not like me! What am I doing wrong?*

But as you grow in love with the other person, you grow in trust that they love just being with you. Your date night doesn't have to blow their socks off. You don't need to receive affirmations from them detailing how funny and unique you are. You just want to be with them and that's enough. The same holds true for our relationship with the Lord.

Fr. Jacques Philippe, in his book *Time for God,* writes, "We pray not to find self-fulfillment or self-satisfaction, but to please God." God doesn't need the most focused and intense prayer. He doesn't need you to say the right things. You don't have to have some sort of emotional high or crystal clear insight. God just needs *you* because you need God. This is what prayer is for. As we give our time to God, he gives us himself in return.

Leaving prayer with a nice insight from scripture is wonderful. That's a gift from the Lord. Leaving prayer feeling joy is awesome. That's another gift. But sometimes leaving prayer feeling absolutely nothing is the greatest gift of all. That means deeper things could be stirring in the recesses of your heart.

And that's a difficult concept to wrap our minds around. Prayer is difficult, but it's absolutely essential. The *Catechism* basically sums up our relationship with Jesus as our prayer (2558). Our prayer is our relationship with Jesus. That's huge. If we are made for an intimate relationship with Jesus, then we are made to pray. We are *praying-beings*. We cannot yada without prayer. We cannot experience all that we are created for without spending time conversing with God.

Prayer is available to all of us anytime because (1) you don't have to know what you're doing, (2) you don't have to do it a certain way, (3) you can be totally real and vulnerable with God, and (4) you don't have to get anything out of it! Anyone can pray because you truly just have to show up. That's also what makes it a challenge—you do have to show up. But when we do show up, we encounter the Lord. We come to know him better, and we feel more and more known. We allow ourselves to be seen, and as we've discussed pretty thoroughly up to this point, that really is the heart of it all.

# ELEVEN

# THE BREATH OF LIFE

My arms wrapped around my knees as I sat in the sand and watched the waves break to the left of the rock jetty. This was my spot. The overcast sky blended into the sea, just the way I liked it. A cool breeze blowing off the water softened the warm air. It was the perfect temperature to wear either shorts or pants. Anything would feel comfortable.

The swell rolling in bounced off the jetty's point, breaking the wave and spilling it over. White foam slowly trickled to the right as the wave approached the shore.

A vacant lifeguard platform stood in the sand to the left of me. Light-blue paint chips curled on its wooden beams. I don't know why I wasn't out in the water. I wanted to be out there, but I was also content right where I was. Sometimes watching the waves can be just as fun as playing in them.

I slowly breathed in the salty air and let out a long exhale. Mist from the breaking waves specked my face. Their crash synced with my breath. In and out. Swell and crash. The seafoam sizzled as the tide left it on the shore.

No one was around—only the ocean and me. Not many people have experienced solitude on these shores. My local spot was far from isolated. In fact, it was one of the more popular tourist destinations in all of Southern California. I scanned my surroundings and enjoyed the bodiless scenery, continuing to take deep, slow breaths all the while.

All of a sudden, the sand crunched behind me, and I looked over my right shoulder. A man walked up and plopped down beside me. I would have been startled if his presence wasn't so calming.

He smiled and took a seat right next to me before I had the chance to say anything. He wrapped his arms around his knees, playfully assuming my posture. It would have been an awkward silence if I didn't feel so enthralled by him. We looked out at the water, and the breeze occasionally brushed his flowing mantle against my leg.

I finally looked back his way, and he slowly turned toward me. His eyes matched the deep gray-blue of the hazy horizon in front of us. I couldn't tell what was the sea, the sky, or his eyes. "I'm proud of you." His words rolled out of his mouth and barrelled into me.

I had no words to return to him. The lump in my throat wouldn't let any sound come out.

We sat there, both soaking in the other's presence.

"OK, Tanner. Slowly open your eyes when you're ready."

I slowly came to. As I wiped tears from my eyes, the seascape in front of me slowly dissolved into my bedroom walls. My seat in the sand congealed into my queen-sized bed. The crash of waves evaporated into the voice of my spiritual director as he wrapped up his meditation.

"Good, good. Thank you for trying that. How was it for you?" Fr. Marvin (his friends called him "Faddah" because of his Hawaiian heritage) smiled encouragingly over FaceTime.

"I feel awkward. Why am I crying?"

Fr. Marvin let out his loud signature laugh. "Don't be weird, dude. It's a gift." He prayed for my upcoming week and for my spiritual protection before hanging up. I dropped my phone onto my bed feeling much more hopeful, much more at peace, and much more alive.

Pope Benedict XVI once taught, "If the lungs of prayer and of the word of God do not nourish the breath of our spiritual life, we risk being overwhelmed by countless everyday things."

During my first year as a FOCUS missionary, Fr. Marvin met with me regularly over the phone. He would pray with me and lead me through various meditations, and I would always walk away from those phone calls feeling like I had taken a deep inhale after a long jog.

I experienced the power of prayer through him—the power of prayer to heal and to help me persevere. My phone calls with Fr. Marvin filled my soul with breath to carry on.

And so I carried on. I continued prioritizing my daily prayer life. Something beautiful happens when you carry on in prayer—something necessary to authentic yada.

By remaining consistent in prayer, we can see the Lord at work in our life. When we stop to pray every day, we can be in tune with the small movements of our heart. We can notice all of the subtle changes in our behavior and outlook. We can see how our prayers get answered (or answered in a different way than we asked for).

Our Lord is constantly at work in our lives, but if we never stop to notice, then we never get to step into all that he offers. You know what they say—if you never stop to smell the roses . . . then the roses . . . might not smell? That's not what they say, but you get my point. Relationships require time. It's simply impossible to have a deep, personal relationship with God if we never spend time with him.

In Exodus 14, Moses parts the Red Sea and God delivers the Israelites from the Egyptians. Pretty wild stuff, right? But after only three days, the Israelites started complaining to Moses about not having enough water. *Three days later*—they start complaining in the very next chapter, Exodus 15!

Now, it's easy to dismiss the Israelites as boneheads or ingrates. (*Ingrate*, by the way, is my mom's favorite term. It's used to denote someone who is ungrateful.) It's easy to think that if we were among the Israelites, we would never behave like that. If we saw God perform such an incredible miracle, we would never doubt him again! Right?

Wrong.

On Easter Sunday, the apostles were found in hiding. After only *three* days, the apostles allowed their fears and doubts to take hold of their situation. These were the people who *lived* with Jesus. They saw him perform miracles. They heard his teaching. They also heard his private teaching, which he only shared with them.

If we do not drink in God's presence on a daily basis, then the anxieties of this world can quickly seem bigger than God (in as few as three days). Prayer is our touchstone for reality. It keeps us grounded in truth and gives us the ability to see the world as it really is.

The Lord moves in our lives in radical ways every day, but the busyness of life keeps time moving. When our day-to-day concerns arise, they can quickly grab hold of our attention. The train of emails, never-ending to-do lists, doctor appointments, groceries, bills, family plans, social events, and all the other daily aspects of life vie for our attention. If we simply move from place to place, activity to activity, person to person without ever pausing to be silent and take in God's work, then it won't take us long to forget about God's presence in our life—just like the Israelites or the apostles.

I can't tell you how many crazy, jaw-dropping encounters with the Lord I've had. I've had so many! I also literally can't tell you about a lot of those times because, well, I just can't remember them.

Before fostering a prayer life, I lived most of my life like Drew Barrymore in *50 First Dates*. If you've never seen the movie, Drew Barrymore plays a young woman who has a severe memory disorder. She basically wakes up thinking that it's the same day every day. Anything new that happens to her is completely wiped away after she falls asleep. Adam Sandler plays a character who falls in love with her, and because of her memory condition, he has to make her fall in love with him every single day—hence the fifty *first* dates from the title.

This is how I lived my life with God. I'd fall in love with him and then completely forget about him the next day. This would happen over and over. And over. I've probably had *fifty thousand* first dates with God.

The Lord lives outside of time and space, but he humbles himself and enters into these dimensions to encounter us. Because of our fickle minds and time's never-ending motion, we can so easily forget these encounters. When we don't stop to pray, the speed of life—especially these days—carries us away.

Praying helps us to remember. In order to know someone, one has to first remember that person. In order to know someone intimately, one has to *relish* that person.

I remember every detail of my first date with Alli. I remember her poofy purple dress. I remember the way she scrunched her face when she smiled at me. I remember the way the sunlight hit her as we sat outside for Mass in the morning. I remember the way the sand felt on my feet as we walked a few steps out into the water later that afternoon. I remember the smell of the random rainstorm that pelted us as we scrambled to find coffee. I remember the taste of the spicy pepperoni pizza that we shared. I remember the song that played in my car when I dropped her off (which later became the song we had our first dance to). I remember all of these vivid details because I sat with them over and over in my mind. They are important to me because she's my wife and the most important woman in the world to me.

If my relationship with God is truly my foundational relationship, then why wouldn't I remember the times he encountered me with similar detail?

In order to yada God deeply, we need to continually recall his work in our lives. The great mystical writers of our faith frequently talk about the need to recollect in order to advance through the spiritual life.

As cute and funny as *50 First Dates* is, it's actually a tragic tale. Adam Sandler's and Drew Barrymore's characters would never be able to experience the depths of intimacy that authentic yada offers, because they couldn't build off their foundation. If you can't remember, then you can't build, and if you can't build, then you can't grow.

I remember my first date with Alli, but I also try to actively remember when she opens up to me about her difficulties so that I can better support her in the future. I try to remember how I make her feel when I mess up or harp on something stupid so that I don't make the same mistake later. I try to remember her hopes and dreams so I can work to support her in building those. I try to remember all the little intricacies of Alli so that we can build a strong, holy, and enjoyable life together. Now, she would probably say that I have the memory of a goldfish, but that's beside the point. I *try*, OK??

Some of the best spiritual advice ever given to me was to plant flag-poles of memories with God in my mind. We need moments that we can look back on and know where we're coming from. When we question where we're going in the future, we can notice the directions the Lord has moved us in the past. We also need moments that we can look back on to know with certainty that God has indeed moved in our lives. Whenever doubts arise or our prayer lives run dry, we can always look to these flagpoles and remember his work. If we can be confident of his past work in our lives, then we can be confident of his future work in our lives.

I remember every detail of this one particular night of prayer with God. I remember walking into the church around 11:00 p.m. after a friend's birthday party. I remember the glow of the red candle next to the tabernacle. I remember being the only one there (besides Jesus). I remember the beanie that I was wearing and took off as I sat on the right side of the aisle in the second pew. I remember sitting with my palms open, desperately open to God's voice. I remember all of these vivid details because I encountered God in that moment. These details are important to me because God is of the utmost importance to me.

I have that experience planted in my memory so I can look back on it and be like, "Yeah, I know the Lord was there with me. I won't forget that. And if he was there with me *then*, then he will be with me *now*." That memory is a well of strength for me that I constantly draw hope from. I reflect on it whenever I need to battle any doubts or difficulties that arise in my life. I remember because I pray, and I continue to pray because I remember.

Of the four habits given to us in Acts 2:42, I would argue that prayer is the hardest one for us to implement today. Our world is increasingly designed to steer us away from silence.

When I first began cultivating my prayer life, I suffered from noise withdrawals—literally. My mind would gravitate toward my to-do list, the weather forecast, an idea I wanted to create, my lunch plans, my weekend plans, my plan to cancel all my plans, etc. My mind still does this when I'm in the middle of a particularly busy stretch, and I know I'm not alone. But can you blame us?

Psychologists describe this distractibility as "hurry sickness"—when your mind is constantly occupied and stimulated, you have withdrawals when you try to slow down. Marketing experts say the average person today sees anywhere from four thousand to ten thousand advertisements every day. Every single day, ninety-five million photos and videos are uploaded to Instagram. We don't know how to *not* be doing something. We live in the loudest, busiest time in the history of humanity, and there is no shortage of distractions to run to.

I have to constantly go to war against that extra ten minutes of sleep, "the scroll," checking just a few more emails, writing or shooting another video, making sure my finances are in order, and on and on. I can fill free time with a seemingly productive activity almost immediately. But sometimes our distractions aren't even within our control. Sometimes we're helpless against the busyness of life, but it all comes down to priorities.

Here's an example from a day that was packed to the brim for Alli and me:

We had to wake up at 3:30 a.m. to park our car at the airport parking lot by 4:30 a.m. From there, we would catch a shuttle to the airport and hopefully make it through security in time to board our flight at 5:20 a.m. Once we landed in Los Angeles at 7:40 a.m., we would have to find an Uber to take us back to my old place in Venice. My old roommates were expecting to see us before I would go teach Alli how to surf. We only had limited time with them because their work day was about to hit full swing and also because my buddy Zach was going to pick us up to take us down to San Clemente. We said our hellos and good-byes before hitting the beach, where Alli was surprisingly a natural at surfing. Zach then swooped in and snagged us, and we set off down south. We had to make it down to San Clemente with enough time to set up the space we had rented out for our film screening later that night. When we arrived at our venue a few hours later, we realized there was a lot more work to do than we had originally anticipated. Thankfully we had arrived with some wiggle room in our schedule. However, what free time remained was quickly consumed with transporting merchandise up and down stairs, putting drinks in coolers, hunting down ice, hanging up photographs, test running the projector and audio, and a whole slew of other activities. When people began trickling in for the event around 6:30 p.m., we realized all that we had eaten that day was an acai bowl. After the event at 9:30 p.m. or so, some friends wanted to grab ice cream with us. When offered ice cream, Alli and I simply don't have the willpower to refuse. We arrived back in Los Angeles later that night around midnight and had to catch a few z's before another early-morning flight back to Denver.

This day trip was about as jam-packed as possible. We were on the move, interacting with other people, or busy working for almost twenty-four hours straight. Or surfing. I guess we did surf for just a little bit.

I know a lot of people can look at this schedule and get it—they might look at this schedule and think that it looks like a cakewalk. Some people reading this might even have days like this *with* kids in tow!

Finding time to pray when we have days like this can seem impossible. I forgot to note that when our plane took off that morning, however, Alli and I had agreed to pray a holy hour during the flight. A "holy air," if you will. We fought to build prayer into our day with the little time we knew we would have.

Prayer can be a challenge, but we have to fight for it. We need to make a determined effort to carve out time to be with God. There will be days when praying seems simply impossible, but that's when we can get creative. Sometimes our prayer can look like a "holy air."

Sometimes it can look like a few moments of silence while nursing a baby. Sometimes it can look like a music-less car ride while driving to and fro doing this and that, working here and running errands over there. The Lord meets us in these moments, and these moments foster yada. They give us spiritual breath that our souls need.

When we pray, we also have to fight through the lack of noise. Our minds will scatter before they settle. We'll hear the voice of all our doubts, confusions, expectations, and desires before we hear the voice of God. But we will hear the voice of God if we persist, and this intimacy will become our center and foundation.

# TWELVE

# "COMPANIONS FOR THE JOURNEY"

When I was a freshman at Houston Baptist University, one of my lifelong friends texted me that her brother, Edwin, was also going to school in Houston. He was apparently studying in Houston's seminary that semester to become a Catholic priest. She encouraged me to reach out to him, so I immediately invited him to lunch. I had never known anyone who wanted to become a priest, and Edwin had definitely never given me priest vibes when we had hung out before. I was curious to hear about what had led to such a big decision.

I was nervous when we met up. Was he going to tell me that I should become a priest, too? Was he going to think that I was a total heathen? But as our conversation unfolded, my tensions eased. He was the same old Edwin—if not an even happier Edwin.

We enjoyed a nice lunch, but I found myself continually distracted by the bracelet he was wearing. Every time he raised his coffee mug for another sip, the black anchor-link chain on his wrist clinked against the ceramic. Clink. Sip. Clink. Sip.

Why an anchor chain? It seemed a little hardcore. He looked like he had broken off some handcuffs. Was this something priests had to wear? It was too distracting after a while for me to not say something.

"What's up, man? You in prison?" I asked. I thought a little joke would open the floor for an explanation. You know, just a little ha-ha.

"I'm sorry?"

"Your wrist. What's up with the chain? You break free?"

He looked down at his wrist. "Oh! This!" He chuckled as he rolled up his sleeves, ensuring that I could get a better view of the full chain. "This is for my Marian consecration."

I didn't know what either of those two words meant by themselves let alone paired together. Marian? Consecration? "Nice. Nice." Our lunch resumed, and I didn't think about his bracelet again. For years . . .

. . . until *I* embarked upon *my* Marian consecration. Enough was enough. I couldn't avoid her any longer.

As I grew more and more in love with God, I had to confront how I actually felt about Mother Mary. She was either a stumbling block to my relationship with Jesus or she was a propeller that would send me closer to him. What she couldn't be was simply a nice devotion, a good person to call on whenever I needed help.

But that's how I had treated her for most of my life. Growing up in the Bible Belt, Mother Mary was a big no-no. She elicited quite the reaction in those around me. Most of my friends growing up were nondenominational, and anything Mary-related was essentially heretical to them. My best friend and I had dozens of arguments over her role within Christianity. I'm talking *passionate* arguments. The idea of two little kids arguing about Mary might sound cute, but these debates were anything but. It's a miracle we're still best friends.

While these arguments never swayed me to ditch Mary outright, they did enough for me to keep Mary at arm's length for most of my life. I held out on fully entrusting myself to her motherly care for twenty-nine years. I loved her, but I didn't trust the desire to love her more. I defended her importance, but I wouldn't dare risk her becoming *too* important in my life. I believed in the power of the Rosary—somewhat. I even prayed it on occasion (mainly when I wanted help booking more acting roles or found myself in relationship difficulties). But the idea of *consecrating myself to Jesus through her*? No thank you. I couldn't do it. That was too far.

But when I moved to Boulder as a FOCUS missionary, I was knee-deep in heartbreak. I was plagued with regrets about how I could have been a better boyfriend. I could have done this, I should have done that. Waves of dread would crash over me. I was entering my thirties, newly single, and had committed to take a break from any romantic relationship for a year. Loneliness pecked at me, and I found myself constantly questioning why God would allow such pain. I missed a strong female presence in my life, and I knew that I needed more strength to pour into the students I was asked to serve. It wasn't fair to them if I was only a shell of myself. Quite frankly, I needed help.

The ache in my heart just kept lingering. Like the marine layer over a Pacific beach town, it just kept clouding over me until my day hit full swing. The sun would peek out for a little bit if I kept busy enough, but by evening it would return and settle over me. No matter what I did, nothing worked. I cried and cried—and cried. I cried more tears than I ever had in my life. Sometimes I would even wake up crying.

And I tried and tried—and tried. I tried to surrender everything to God. I tried practicing the four habits like I never had before. I learned more about our faith. I spent more time with friends and made sure to catch up with old ones. I started seeing both a therapist and a spiritual director. I made sure I went to Confession frequently and daily Mass. I didn't miss one minute of my daily holy hours. And yet, despite all the work I was putting into my spiritual life, I felt like I was still holding back ever so slightly.

After a few weeks in Boulder, I noticed a bunch of people within my campus ministry wearing the same anchor-link chain bracelet that Edwin (now *Fr.* Edwin) had worn during our lunch so many years ago. It was almost laughable. I heard them clinking everywhere I went.

I finally asked someone what was up with the handcuffs people were wearing. "This is what a lot of people wear after they make a Marian consecration," they replied. The people I noticed wearing this chain were all people whose faith was contagious. They seemed to be in love with Jesus, and I could tell that they knew him well based on my conversations with them. I finally accepted that I had one glaring hole left in my relationship with God—surrendering to his mother's care.

The idea of a Marian consecration seemed much less scary than it would have growing up. It helped that I finally knew what those two words meant—an act of entrusting one's life and everything one has (a *consecration*) to Jesus through his Blessed Virgin Mother.

God entrusted himself to Mary, so why couldn't I? He not only trusted her to say yes to his will (what if she had said no?!), but he planted himself in her womb! He was a *zygote* in her! Babies are 100 percent dependent on their mothers—completely. If God himself depended 100 percent on Mother Mary, why wouldn't *I* do the same? The greatest saints have been dependent upon her, so why wouldn't I follow their lead?

As I mulled over the idea of doing a Marian consecration, I thought back to what Sr. Ruth taught me so long ago: The saints loved Mary. Sr. Ruth had passed away at this point, but her words lived on in me.

I loved the saints. They helped me tremendously in my faith journey. I wanted to become a saint one day. "The saints loved Mary."

I opened my Bible to the gospels before making my decision. I wanted to read what was written about her one more time—just to make sure no red flags stood out.

And in everything I read, scripture portrayed Mary in only the most brilliant light. Some of Jesus's last words, words that he squeezed out of suffocating lungs, were used to give his mother to humanity. Think about that. He could have said *anything* or *nothing*. Nothing would have been a very appropriate response! We wouldn't be reading the Bible today and thinking, "Ugh! Why didn't he say something when he was dying?" How painful those words must have been for his failing respiratory system.

But he *did* say something. In the climax of human history, Jesus said, "Woman, behold your son." And then to John he said, "Behold your mother." When he called Mary "woman," he wasn't dishonoring her like my friends in Dallas had argued when we were growing up. Just the opposite, in fact: he was alluding to Eve—the original "woman" and mother of all. He was declaring Mary as the *new* mother of all. He was bestowing upon her the *ultimate* honor.

God wants us to be in his mother's care, just like he was. It's part of his design. It's actually *necessary* for deeper yada. In holding back from Mother Mary, I was holding back from God. I had to finally face her.

So I picked up Fr. Michael Gaitley's *33 Days to Morning Glory* and started the process of consecrating myself. (There are various Marian consecrations one can make, but *33 Days to Morning Glory* is very simple and, as the name implies, only takes thirty-three days to complete.) I looked thirty-three days ahead on the calendar, and I noticed that I would complete my consecration on the feast of Our Lady of Sorrows, a special day that honors Mother Mary.

On my second-to-last day of the thirty-three-day "retreat," I went for a jog in the mountains. (I say "retreat" because it's just a few readings and prayers every day. It really is super simple!)

One of my favorite things to do at the time was going on a run into the Flatirons and finding the most secluded place to pray. So I set off. The only trail I followed was the trail no one else was on. When I trekked deep enough into the mountains to get away from people and high enough to have a solid view, I climbed to the top of a rock. Its bowl-like top was perfect to sit in and bask in the sunshine. It was like a hot tub without any water.

When I lived in California, my roommates and I basically lived without shirts on. When I transitioned to missionary life, though, I was quickly told that being shirtless all the time wasn't the most modest thing in the world. I missed the sun on my skin, so I took off my shirt and listened to whatever sad-boy music my Spotify threw at me, soaking it all in. All the sun, all the feels, all the beauty. After a while, I felt like I should take my earbuds out and truly bathe in the moment. All the silence, all the warmth, all of God's creation.

I closed my eyes and allowed the peace of the moment to quiet my mind. I was going to begin praying, but a loud flutter drew my eyes open. A beautiful blue bird flew around me. It seemed to dance as it hovered to and fro before eventually flying off. And then another one flew by me. And another. One by one, bright-blue birds circled around me and flew off. I counted seven total. They were so jarringly blue against the green backdrop of the pines, and they were so surprisingly close to me. Even with all the space around . . .

It felt too special to have just been a coincidence. I felt an increasing urge to look up the biblical symbolism of blue birds, so I pulled out my phone and Googled "birds symbolism in Bible." There were a few articles but nothing with a clear answer. Birds apparently have a wide array of meanings in the Bible. My mind kept thinking back to the Holy Spirit in the form of a dove, when it hit me.

Blue is the color commonly attributed to our Blessed Virgin Mother. Tears immediately filled my eyes as I realized that on the eve of the Feast of Our Lady of Sorrows, Mother Mary sent me seven blue birds—one for each of her seven sorrows.

Traditionally, the Catholic Church has described these as the seven sorrows of Mary:

1. The prophecy of the priest, Simeon (Lk 2:34–35)
2. The flight into Egypt (Mt 2:13–21)
3. The child Jesus is lost for three days and found in the Temple (Lk 2:41–50)
4. Mary meets Jesus as he carries his cross to Calvary (Jn 19:17)
5. The Crucifixion and death of Jesus (Jn 19:18–30)
6. Jesus is taken down from the Cross and given to his mother (Jn 19:39–40)
7. Jesus is laid in the tomb (Jn 19:39–42)

Seven sorrows. Seven blue birds. I felt a sense that Mary was showing me that Jesus would make all of my struggles into something beautiful. She was next to God, gazing at me in this tiny snow globe we call Earth. She was welcoming me into the Holy Family in a deeper, more profound way. When I was as lonely as I've ever been, she showed me that I've gained another family member.

I sat there and rested in the consolation of knowing that I was cared for. Consolations come far and few in between, but they're oh so sweet when they happen. After a while, I put my earbuds back in, switched my playlist from sad-boy folk to something more upbeat, and then jogged off.

Now, could I be reading too far into a flock of birds? Sure. Regardless, those birds gave me such hope in a time when I really needed it. After I completed my consecration, I felt as close to Mother Mary as I ever had, and I don't think it's a coincidence that I also felt as close to Jesus as I ever had. I felt more familiar, more *familial* with him than I ever had. I understood him on a different level. I felt deeper yada.

Following my consecration, Jesus did slowly bring joy to my sorrows, fruit from my pain. My emotions and my will slowly but radically transformed. It was not overnight (far from it), but the Lord did eventually bring healing into parts of my heart that I thought were beyond repair.

It's fairly simple. If we are made to yada Jesus, then we need to draw close to his mother—the one among us who knew him best. If we are made for intimacy with God, then we are made for intimacy with all of his loved ones, and as we all know, there's no love like that between a man and his mother.

If you truly desire intimacy with the Lord and want to step into the life that you were designed to live, then the four habits of Acts 2:42 are essential. However, your heart will still be found lacking until you hand everything over to Mother Mary.

Likewise, if we are made to be in communion with God, then we are made to be in communion with those who are also in communion with him. This includes Mother Mary and all of our fellow brothers and sisters who are actively seeking to grow close to Jesus. This also includes all of those who have passed from this life to the next. If you truly desire the fullness of yada, then the Communion of Saints will help you.

The saints are those people in heaven—officially canonized or not—who are in eternal communion with God. And because God "is not God of the dead, but of the living" (Mk 12:27), the saints are a living community. They are our brothers and sisters as well! They are our companions for our journeys on earth, helping us to draw into greater yada with our Lord.

When we look to the saints for help, we can grow closer to God. Just as I did with Mother Mary, I used to keep the saints an arm's length away. I thought they were cool, insightful even, but not people I could actually relate to. As I continued to dive deeper with God, however, I found myself desiring the saints' help more and more. My desires grew from wanting to learn from them to wanting to imitate them. I began to view them less as enlightened sages and more as real friends who want to help me.

The saints have been a vital part of my marriage with Alli. I first made up my mind that I wanted to date Alli when she explained to me that she asks a different saint to intercede for each of her family members. (Yes, I am fully aware that I sound like a total Catholic nerd, but I don't care.) At our reception after our wedding, we organized our seating chart by different saints. There was the St. Joseph table, the St. Thérèse of Lisieux table, the St. Ignatius of Loyola table, and on and on.

St. Thérèse is Alli's Confirmation saint (and her feast day shares Alli's birthday), and St. Ignatius of Loyola is my Confirmation saint. Leading up to our wedding day, Alli and I asked for the intercession of both St. Thérèse of Lisieux and St. Ignatius of Loyola every day. We asked them to pray for a holy and saintly marriage for us.

There is a tradition around St. Thérèse that she sends roses to people who ask for her intercession, as a sign of letting that person know their prayers were heard by God. Usually people will pray a novena (a nine-day prayer) to her and receive a rose on the ninth and final day. I think Catholics can sometimes get superstitious about it, but St. Thérèse *did* promise, "I will send down a shower of roses from the heavens; I will spend my heaven doing good upon earth."

Alli and I weren't praying a novena to St. Thérèse, and we weren't expecting any sort of sign from her. We just really loved asking St. Thérèse to pray for us.

There were obviously plenty of roses on our wedding day, so we didn't think much of anything at first. That would have been ridiculous.

We also didn't think much of a priest friend reaching out to us and telling us that he had a dream we were in. In this dream, there were pink roses on the ground leading up to the stairs where Alli and I were living. He told it in a humorous way, so I laughed and carried on—though I probably should have listened more, because this priest received his call to the priesthood through a dream. The Lord very clearly worked in this man's sleep.

But when Alli and I went on our honeymoon in an artsy little town in Baja Mexico, there were pink roses *everywhere*. There were pink rosebushes leading up to our Airbnb. Pink roses *in* our Airbnb. Pink roses at our table for dinner. Pink roses painted in murals along the streets we walked. We finally started to take notice and put two and two together.

It seemed like an excessive number of roses. Too many to be coincidental at the very least. Either this town was obsessed with roses or we were playing tricks in our minds. And then it hit me after Mass on our way to the beach. My last name, Kalina, has Czech origins that translate to "guelder rose." *Kalina* is also referred to as a type of flower in many other languages. We had a deep sense that St. Thérèse was letting us know that God heard our prayers. With Alli becoming a new Kalina, God was giving both of us a rose forever.

To yada God is to embrace all of God. This includes all of his loved ones. To yada God is to embrace the full family of God, the Communion of Saints.

Once we die, we will (God willing) go to heaven and fall into the fullest form of yada. And true, authentic yada seeks to expand. The saints love God so much that they continue working to build his kingdom once they're in heaven. The saints want to help us get to heaven! They play an integral part in our relationship with the Lord.

When Alli and I came to that realization about our last name, Kalina, I felt an overwhelming rush of gratitude and love for the Lord. I felt like he cared about my marriage and that he was blessing it. I felt confident that I was doing his will, and I attribute St. Thérèse's prayers with helping me achieve that.

(On a side note, to kind of break the fourth wall here, as I'm writing this my mom just sent Alli a flower delivery. Alli was in the hospital for some health reasons, and my mom wanted to treat her to make her feel better. Guess what was in the vase? Roses and guelder roses. I kid you not. St. Thérèse is a wild woman. OK, back to your regularly scheduled broadcast.)

I've always felt a draw to St. Ignatius of Loyola. Maybe because I went to a Jesuit high school. Maybe because he wrote some fire quotes. Whatever the case, as I've grown older I've been continually astounded at how similar our paths have been. (I'm not saying I'm as virtuous or as holy as he was—just that our lives have traveled down similar roads.)

St. Ignatius grew up with dreams of becoming one of the greatest knights Spain had ever seen. He wanted to be a star. Likewise, I dreamed of becoming a baseball star and a movie star. St. Ignatius got close to his dreams becoming a reality until a cannonball to the leg wrecked them. Likewise, I got close to my dreams becoming a reality until bullying came in like a cannonball and wrecked them. As St. Ignatius lay recovering from his broken leg and broken heart, he experienced a radical reversion to his Catholic faith. Likewise, as I lay in Los Angeles recovering from broken dreams and a broken heart,

I experienced a radical reversion to my Catholic faith. St. Ignatius decided to give everything to God around the age of thirty. Likewise, I decided to leave Los Angeles and my dreams behind just before my thirtieth birthday. St. Ignatius went to college shortly after that, rooming with two other young college-aged men. Likewise, I became a campus missionary and shared life with younger college-aged men. St. Ignatius struggled with scrupulosity throughout his life. Likewise, I have and sometimes continue to struggle with scrupulosity. St. Ignatius wrote books and letters that have helped countless Catholics for centuries. Likewise, I'm writing a book that, at the very minimum, you and my mom are reading.

St. Ignatius has consistently inspired me to grow closer to the Lord. I know that he is my Confirmation saint for a reason, and I know that his intimacy with God in heaven is continuously seeking to expand, aspiring to bring me into the fold as well.

The saints are our spiritual friends. If you want to grow in intimacy with the Lord, in deeper and deeper yada, then pick a saint or two to learn from and to pray for you. They will only help your relationship with the Lord.

# THIRTEEN

# AN INVITATION

In middle school, one of my good friends gave me a book for Christmas. It had a tattered brown cover and rough, untrimmed edges. I liked the way it felt in my hands.

My friend was nondenominational, and the book she gave me was apparently the hip new book in her church circles. It detailed all of the wild stories of a missionary and his various encounters during years of evangelizing the homeless.

I devoured every page of that book. I couldn't believe how crazy the writer was. His escapades seemed straight out of a movie, and he wrote with such joy and clarity. And humor! He seemed like the kind of guy I would want to grab a beer with—even though I had no idea what beer tasted like at that point in my life. Regardless, I wanted to live like him.

My excitement bubbled after reading the final lines of the last page. I sat outside my mom's parish office, waiting for her to get off work. My feet tapped as I looked around to see if anyone was nearby. I wanted to share what I had read about with someone, with anyone! But the church hallways were vacant. I gave it a few more minutes before finally slamming the book shut and bursting into my mom's office. "Mom, I think I want to evangelize."

"That's great, sweetie." My mom's eyes remained glued to her computer screen.

"Mom, did you hear me? I want to evangelize!"

"You want an angel what now?" Her brow furrowed as she leaned closer to her screen.

"No, Tina. I think he said he wants to *evangelize*." The lady who shared a desk next to my mom chuckled.

"What does that mean to you, Tanner?" My mom took her eyes off her screen and looked at me.

"I want to be an evangelist!" I held up the book. My mom looked at it and then back to me.

"Like you want to be an evangelical?"

I didn't know what an evangelical was, but I assumed it was someone who evangelized. ". . . Yeah. Sure. I just want to do what this guy does." I tried gesturing for my mom to grab the book in my hands, but she wouldn't budge. The tattered brown cover looked even more tattered as she spun her chair back toward her computer.

"No, Tanner. We're Catholic. We don't do that."

"What do you mean?"

"We're not evangelical. We're *Catholic*."

"Well, why can't—"

"Do you want to show that book to Sr. Ruth?"

". . . No."

"I'll go get her. Do you want her to see that? I'm sure she'd have some things to say."

"No, it's fine. Never mind." I dropped the book to my side and hung my head as I walked out of her office.

I wish I would have let my mom show that book to Sr. Ruth. I wish I would have let her ask Sister about evangelizing. I know that it would have brought clarification to any confusion between us. I wasn't trying to convert to evangelical Christianity. I just wanted to spread the Gospel.

But instead of pushing my mom further, I sat back down outside of her office and went a full decade believing that Catholicism and evangelizing were two incompatible practices.

It wasn't until college that I learned just the opposite is true. In fact, the Catholic Church teaches—and has always taught—that "the task of evangelizing all people constitutes *the essential mission of the Church. . . .* Evangelizing is in fact the grace and vocation proper to the Church, her deepest identity. *She exists in order to evangelize . . .*" (emphasis mine).

The whole purpose of the Catholic Church is to evangelize! To fully experience yada, we have to bring others into the intimacy we've discovered. Love seeks to expand. This is why God is a holy *Trinity*. The love between the Father and the Son is so palpable that another person exists—the Holy Spirit. The love between persons must flow out to others. This is why the core purpose of marriage is to raise families. The love between a husband and wife is designed to be so palpable that another person is created.

Whereas sin and death seek to divide people, true yada seeks to unite.

The more I fell in love with God during my time in Los Angeles, the more I wanted to lay down my life for others. As Jesus himself put it, "For whoever would save his life will lose it; and whoever loses his life for my sake, he will save it" (Lk 9:24). Or as St. Catherine of Siena put it, "One who knows more loves more."

Our intimacy with God is meant to overflow out to others. We experience yada with God more fully when we help others experience yada with God. It's one of the great paradoxes of our faith. The more we give away, the more we receive. Moreover, the more we give away, the more we *want* to give away. But we'll never want to do that if we keep everything to ourselves.

If we want to experience all that our hearts are made for, then we have to give our hearts away. When we lay down our lives, then and only then do we live life to the fullest. This was never made more clear to me than during my first few weeks as a FOCUS missionary.

Our culture loves birthdays. They're basically an excuse to have a day when you can do whatever you want with whomever you want wherever you want. My own birthday has always felt like a bit of a drag, however. I've always found it to be the most underwhelming day of the year, and I blame the date—August 20. A late August birthday was the worst day to have a birthday as a kid because it always fell around the first day of school. A new class with new people in a new environment doesn't exactly bode well for having a big ol' bash. It's awkward getting people who barely know you to come together and celebrate your life. "Hey, class! It's Tanner's birthday today!" "Who?" "Tanner! The boy sitting next to you!" "Oh."

My first birthday as a FOCUS missionary felt eerily similar to the birthdays I had growing up. I was still new to Boulder so I didn't really know anyone all that well, and classes had just begun a few days before so people were busy doing their own thing.

I awoke to a scroll of texts from my friends and family: "Happy Bday, T! I hope it's LIT, bruddah!" "Happy birthday, bro! Wish I could celebrate with you today, but I know you'll make it a good one!!" "HBD

TK, feel the love today!" "Dude! It's your birthday! Don't get too cray lol!"

They were really kind messages, but everyone's assumption that I had friends to celebrate with only made me feel lonelier. Based on people's texts, it seemed like I should be doing something exciting with my day, so I felt lame that all I had planned was a full day of work. I stuffed my phone in my backpack and made a commitment not to check it anymore.

When I drove up to the Catholic Center, I half hoped that someone would pop out and surprise me with a "Happy birthday!" When no one did, I felt a tinge of disappointment. "Ready to chalk?" A student patted me on the back, handed me a bag of chalk, and walked off. I watched them round the corner and then looked down at the bag in my hands.

Every year for the first week of class, the Catholic ministry at the University of Colorado celebrates a big Mass to welcome the returning students and incoming freshmen. Fr. Peter, in his mastery of all things random, would train students in the art of making sidewalk chalk. (He swore it would save money to make the chalk ourselves, but I think it actually cost way more than buying chalk in bulk straight from a store—I think FP just liked bringing students together to get their hands dirty.)

The annual chalk mission is to let every single soul on campus know about the welcome Mass. Sometimes all we can do as missionaries is invite others. We can't force them to come. But if we can invite, then we should really *invite*.

I took a deep breath and crossed the street to begin chalking CU's entire campus. A large group of students and I had already spent the previous few days on our hands and knees, covering CU's grounds and advertising for the upcoming welcome Mass. A late-night rainstorm, however, washed away our week's worth of work. Needless to say, we had a tall task ahead of us. If we wanted students to know about the welcome Mass, then we had to retrace all our steps.

While most of the things we wrote with chalk were relatively simple and quick—"Welcome Mass! 7:00 p.m.! Sunday! @ St. Thomas Aquinas!"—a team of us spent some time earlier in the week making a large and elaborate drawing to catch people's attention. Because of the rainstorm the night before, it was an indiscernible mess. When I walked up to it, I got down on my knees, whipped out a stick of neon-green chalk, and began tracing over what parts I could recognize. My knees were raw from the hours of rubbing against cement throughout the week.

Students walked by while I worked. Some paid no attention to me while others discreetly snickered and pointed. I kept my head down and whipped out a purple chalk stick. There I was, turning twenty-nine years old, by myself in a new town, on my hands and bloodied knees, drawing with sidewalk chalk and getting ridiculed by eighteen-year-olds. I was forlorn, frustrated, and above all, embarrassed. My birthday was anything but "lit."

I dusted off my chalky hands on my shorts and rose from my squat. My back ached as I stretched it out. I wanted to give my life away for others, but not like this. I wanted it to be *fun*. I wanted it to look like I had imagined it to look.

But then I remembered what Paul wrote to the Philippians: "Christ Jesus, who, though he was in the form of God, did not count equality with God a thing to be grasped, but emptied himself, taking the form of a servant, being born in the likeness of men. And being found in human form he humbled himself and became obedient unto death, even death on a cross" (2:5–8).

I looked at the drawing I had salvaged—a massive, colorful cross. The Lord was giving me a birthday gift. He was giving me the chance to evangelize. It wasn't the gift I imagined, but it was the gift I asked for—kind of like when you ask for clothes for Christmas and your mom ends up getting you an egregious number of waffle henley shirts. (Thank you, Mom, for your gifts. I cherish them.) Who was I to complain that the Lord gave me what I asked for?

I spent the rest of the morning chalking even more areas than I had originally covered throughout the week. I was determined. As silly as chalking a campus was on my birthday, it really was an opportunity that could lead others to Christ. Someone could see something I wrote and give Mass a chance. That person's life could forever change. That person's *soul* could forever change.

As C. S. Lewis once wrote, "You have never talked to a mere mortal." Everyone you have talked to has an eternal destiny. Our goal should be getting everyone to heaven. If chalking could help that, then so be it.

Later that night, my team of FOCUS missionaries rounded me up and drove me to Denver to celebrate my birthday at a cool food hall downtown. Even though they didn't really know me just yet, they celebrated me and made me feel loved. The Lord was giving me another birthday gift. This one, too, wasn't the gift I imagined, but it was the gift I desired—kind of like a glossy new surfboard under the Christmas tree on Christmas morning. (I've never actually received a new surfboard for Christmas, but Mom, if you're reading this . . .) Lesson learned: the Lord is never outdone in generosity.

The work of evangelization is for all of us. It's not always glamorous. In fact, it rarely is. It never looks like we imagine it will look. But we are each called to "go therefore and make disciples of all nations" (Mt 28:19). That call is not just for our priests or religious sisters. It's not just for our missionaries or church ladies. It's for every single one of us who has received the grace of Baptism.

To know love is to become love. "Love does not stay idle," as St. Catherine of Siena wrote. To know love—to know the God who is love—is to be filled with a raging fire that needs to spread in order to stay alive. If we don't bring that fire more fuel, then it slowly dies.

And I know that the idea of evangelizing can seem daunting or scary. Where does one even begin? How can we share our faith if it's not a part of our job?

We don't have to go to a far-off country, or even into unknown neighborhoods, in order to evangelize. God has placed people in our lives for a reason—the neighbors we have, the coworkers we work with, the friends we spend time with. While not all of us are asked to officially become missionaries or employees of the Church, we *are* all asked to become missionaries wherever we are.

And that can be super simple: we can host people for dinner and share a meal, we can introduce ourselves to people after Mass or when we walk by them in our neighborhood, we can have spiritual conversations with people whose trust we've earned. We can do a million different things.

One of the biggest things we can do is simply offer an invitation. How many times have your weekend plans changed on a dime simply because someone invited you somewhere or to do something? An invitation always incites a reaction. When Jesus gathered his disciples to follow him, he always began with an invitation. When it comes to evangelizing, we can put so much pressure on ourselves. Really, all we need is to simply be bold enough to invite. The Lord often takes it from there.

I've had guys reach out to me *years* after talking to them and say that introducing myself to them or simply inviting them to something stuck with them. You never know the seeds you plant that the Lord will cause to grow in their own time.

Invite people to Mass with you. Invite people to pray with you. Invite people to spend time with you and other believers. I'm inviting you to go and invite others! (See what I did there?)

# FOURTEEN

# YADA YADA YADA

I was completely stunned. There was no way he had a *royal* flush!

My mouth hung open as he wrapped his arms around all of my chips and slid them to his side of the table. I watched his hands sort through my chips and stack them in little towers according to their color. Welp, there went my twenty bucks.

I had a straight flush, the second-strongest possible hand one could have. Straight flushes are so rare that no one ever thinks about someone having a *royal* flush (the strongest possible hand to have). Royal flushes are so incredibly rare that they're not even a thought. I felt more than confident going all in. I had the game in the bag!

But nope. The student in front of me had pulled off the near impossible. Just to put this in perspective, the odds of being struck by lightning are 1 in 15,300. The odds of someone having a royal flush in a game of Texas Hold'em are 1 in 649,739. Someone could play Texas Hold'em every day of their life for ten lifetimes and never see a royal flush.

I watched the group of students huddled around my table finish the game, occasionally getting up to fetch someone more pizza or water. I cheered for Heston, the one student I knew somewhat decently. Heston was in my Bible study, a senior football player, and one of the guys I was really trying to invest in. I prayed for him every day by name for a year.

I wanted him to catch fire with his faith. I knew it was in him, and I knew he was struggling. During Bible study, I could tell that things were clicking with him, but when I would ask if he had made it to Mass the Sunday before, I'd get met with the same shrug of his shoulders each week. I knew that Bible study alone wasn't going to be enough for him to fall in love with God.

So I started inviting him to other things—lunch on campus, coffee, or poker. I knew that poker was his favorite thing to do, so I planned a big poker night at my house. I picked up a variety of pizzas during the day and cooked them to be ready as people started trickling in. Heston told me another football player or two would join, so I was excited to meet some more student-athletes.

"Hey man, you cool if I hang with Charlie?"

I looked at Heston's friend. There was no way he was asking what I thought he was asking. "I'm sorry?"

"Blow, bro. Can I do some blow?" His friend didn't beat around the bush. He wanted to see if he could do cocaine. I guess he was just going to whip it out then and there if I agreed to it.

"Nah man. I'm not cool with that." I looked at Heston. He looked back at me and gave me his signature shrug. I could tell he was just as surprised as well.

That night did a lot to build trust and rapport with Heston. His attendance at Bible study was much more frequent afterward, and he was much more responsive to my invitations to do other things. I didn't win poker night, but I won something even more valuable. I won over Heston.

I continued to lead Heston in Bible study, and when he graduated, I called him on a couple occasions just to check in and hear how life was treating him.

Almost two years after he graduated, when I was done being a FOCUS missionary, he reached out to me to grab coffee. He told me he wanted to dive into his faith and that our friendship and Bible study in Boulder had planted a lot of seeds in him. Heston has since become a solid friend and a solid disciple of Christ, even helping lead others in their faith journeys. He went from "cocaine poker nights" to being a confident disciple of Christ. I'm proud of him, and I'm grateful to have been a small part of his journey.

My relationship with Heston started as a simple succession of invitations: invitations to Bible study, invitations to lunch, invitations to poker, etc. But there is a more methodical approach to evangelization. My relationship with Heston is a classic example of win-build-send.

I hesitate to say "method," much less describe one, because it can seem disingenuous, but this is simply mirroring what Jesus did with his twelve disciples. In order to save the world, Jesus could have come down in thunder and lightning or any other form he wanted. Instead, he won twelve guys over, built them up to spread his message, and then sent them to do just that. That's all win-build-send is. I've also heard parishes describe this method as bring-grow-send. Whatever you want to call it, evangelization looks like an invitation, followed by friendship, followed by spiritual investment, followed by sending them to do likewise.

This whole book is structured around this method. I hopefully won you over (at least enough for you to continue reading all the way to the very end!), and successfully shared what I've learned spiritually—now I am sending you to go and do likewise.

Yada with God yearns to expand. And here's the cool thing: when we share our faith, our faith strengthens. Yada seeks to expand, and as it expands, yada deepens. They say the best way to learn is to teach. Sometimes the best way to grow in your relationship with God is to share about your relationship with God!

Something happens when we evangelize. The fire in our heart gets stoked. One of the surest ways to grow cold in our faith is to be chill about sharing our faith. When we share our faith, however, our longing for intimacy with God grows, as does our heart's *capacity* for intimacy with God. We can experience deeper yada. And if we continue daring to grow closer to God, he fills our hearts so that we can overflow to even more people.

One of my acting buddies from Los Angeles, Juston, was also a college athlete. Juston played baseball at my alma mater, the University of Texas at Austin. He followed in the footsteps of his brother and father, who also played baseball at UT. In fact, his father, James, was a two-sport star at UT. He quarterbacked the Longhorns' 1969 National Championship team.

James passed away when Juston was a teen. After his baseball career at UT and entering the entertainment industry, Juston received the chance of a lifetime. He was cast in the role of his father in a film about a player on that 1969 Texas football team. He got to suit up and wear his father's uniform, talk like his father, look like his father, and act like his father. I got teary-eyed when Juston first explained to me what it felt like performing in that role. I know that it was a transformative experience for him.

Every single one of us is called to "wear our father's uniform." St. John Paul II once taught, "No believer in Christ . . . can avoid this supreme duty: to proclaim Christ to all peoples." We are called to talk like God our Father, look like him, and act like him to the world. I'm convinced that we are called to proclaim Christ not because we need to increase the number of people in church pews, but because this is the way to increase our own hearts' capacity to yada. When we do our Father's work, we grow closer to him—and the best way to do the Father's work is to follow Jesus, who did it best. When we share our faith with others, we transform. We step into our inheritance. We experience the fullness of yada, the fullness of what our hearts ache for.

If this is intimidating to you, I invite you to begin with a meal. The Bible opens and closes with a meal. The source and summit of our faith—the Eucharistic sacrifice—is a meal. The Lord does big things in the context of meals, so I invite you to invite someone for a meal and then go from there. Bring the Lord into your conversation whenever it's natural to do so, and continue reaching out to whomever you dine with afterward.

Even if it's a total disaster, the Lord can move through it. The first meal in the Bible (the fall of Adam and Eve) led to a lot of turmoil, but the Lord entered into that brokenness with us to bring about the beautiful story of salvation. He enters into and heals our broken humanity in the Eucharistic meal every day. He can use our broken meals as well to bring others into communion with him. It's kind of his forte.

"Not all of us can do great things, but we can do small things with great love," as Mother Teresa once taught. When we yada God, the Lord can use a simple meal or conversation to change the course of someone's life for all of eternity. This is what Jesus did. Throughout the gospels, he was constantly at table with people sharing a meal with them. Simply being next to the divine fire in his heart was enough to set people ablaze. The same is true with us. When we yada God, the divine flame in our hearts *will* catch others on fire. We simply have to create situations for that to happen. Even if our conversations go no deeper than the "yada yada yada" of everyday life, people will get a sense that we're different because we yada.

We are created for intimacy. Let's give that intimacy a real shot—and once we've tasted its goodness, let's allow others to feast.

# CONCLUSION

Paragraph 2014 of the *Catechism of the Catholic Church* says, "Spiritual progress tends toward ever more intimate union with Christ." That paragraph continues, "God calls us all to this intimate union with him . . ."

God calls us *all* to this intimate union with him.

This is what we are made for. Every single one of us. This is our design. We are made to know and be known on the deepest levels of our being. We are made for yada.

As this book concludes, I invite you to seriously consider how you can dive deeper into this great adventure. I invite you to share in God's own blessed life. I invite you to step into all that you were created for.

And I want to be up front. This invitation is not an invitation to an easy life. Far from it. This is, however, an invitation to a *full* life.

It's important to note that our culture does not view reality through this lens. Our world does not believe that we were created for an intimate union with Christ.

Our society today says that we're all just a bunch of Chipotle bowls— we can design our own paths. We can throw a little bit of this in there if we want it, a little bit of that, toss some pico on the side and throw a wad of guacamole on top—boom, we're set. Heck, if we want to be a burrito, then we can be a burrito.

(Quick Chipotle tip: Always choose a burrito bowl. If you were hankering for a burrito, then get a free tortilla on the side. But fill up your bowl regardless. Burrito bowls come with way more food. You can make your own burrito if you want, and you'll have food left over if you do. It's a cheat. You'll thank me later. End tangent.)

Our culture simply does not care about any of this. And yet, it recognizes the deep ache to know and be known that every single one of us experiences. Our world recognizes the human heart's longing and offers an infinite number of solutions to fill that longing. Ironically, God (the One who *is* infinite) is never one of those solutions. Finding God in all the noise can be difficult, and in my opinion, this is really the first big hurdle to jump over if you want to experience yada.

My friend, if you want to step into your design and all that you are made for, your journey needs to start with a firm act of your will. Accept the fact that you're going to see the world differently. Accept the fact that you might be considered odd to the world in certain areas of your life. Accept it and then *dive in*.

And don't look back. Step out into the deep, covenantal, life-giving relationship with Christ that he offers you. Step into yada.

With this book, I've done my best to share with you how I've gone about responding to this call. I'll admit that at times, it hasn't looked pretty. At other times, it's been glorious. Whatever the case, it'll always be an ongoing process. I'm trying to constantly go deeper, and I invite you to join me.

I've also tried to share with you how the four habits of Acts 2:42 have helped me grow in intimacy with God—along with the help of Mother Mary and the saints. I've also shared how, once I developed intimacy with God, I felt the draw to bring others into intimacy with him. This is how we do it! This is what yada looks like practically.

I'll leave you with one more quick story. So a while back I was taking a girl out for dates. We were hitting it off and spending a lot of time together. I thought she was super interesting, and it was clear she thought the same about me. From my vantage point, she was my girlfriend. Our relationship had reached that point in which it would be super weird if I took another girl out on a date, and I would have been pretty devastated if she went on a date with another guy.

So when I dropped her off at her car one day, I tried to charmingly drop the status-bomb. "Hey, you're not a bad girlfriend." She raised her eyes from her tangled keychain, and I gave her a playful grin. I thought I was being suave. I was feeling pretty good about myself.

But then she was like, "Woah, woah, woah. What did you say?"

"I said . . . you're . . . a good girlfriend . . . ? Eh heh? . . . ?" I tried holding my grin.

"Girlfriend? You think I'm your *girlfriend*?"

The rest of our conversation got real awkward real fast. Lesson learned: as a man, I should always be clear with where I thought a relationship stood. Making assumptions about being on the same page is not cool. She was right in calling me out.

Another lesson learned: I can perceive a relationship with someone to be one thing, while that person can perceive it to be a completely different thing. I thought I was in a committed relationship, a done deal, and she clearly did not.

The same can be true for our relationship with Jesus. We might think our relationship with Jesus is one thing, while in actuality it's a completely different thing.

We might want a relationship with Jesus but on our own terms. We might even try to make our relationship with Jesus look and feel comfortable and easy. However, a relationship is a two-way street. There are certain things that are required from both parties for a relationship to remain healthy and intimate. Otherwise, that relationship is more of an acquaintanceship than an actual relationship. Your relationship with an acquaintance can look however you want it to look. Your relationship with a lover cannot. Your relationship with Love himself requires certain things from you—not in a legalistic, demanding way, but in a committed, life-giving way.

As a young lad, I spent a lot of time enacting the disciplines of being in a relationship with Jesus without fostering an actual relationship with him. As I've hopefully drilled home in this book by now, discipline without relationship ends up in burnout. I've also spent a good portion of my life *wanting* a relationship with Jesus but without practicing any sort of discipline in that relationship. Relationships without discipline end up in rebellion.

We are created for intimacy with God, for yada, and we experience that intimacy through the four habits of Acts 2:42—the teaching of the Church, fellowship, the sacraments, and prayer. Everything in the spiritual life is so interconnected.

We simply cannot have the deep, heart-satisfying kind of intimacy that we long for without discipline, and we cannot practice any sort of discipline without the goal of greater and greater intimacy. On a similar note, we cannot have deeper intimacy with God without relating to Mother Mary and the Communion of Saints, and we cannot relate to Mother Mary and the saints without the goal of deeper intimacy with God!

And once we live in deep intimacy with the Lord, we have to be on mission and share it. We simply cannot have intimacy without mission, and we cannot be on mission without intimacy. Everything is so intertwined and geared toward greater yada with God. We cannot isolate any one part of the spiritual life. This is what we are made for. This is holiness.

We are made for it all. We are made to be drenched in the love of God, not to sprinkle his presence through our lives here and there. We are made to *soak* him in. But we need to dive into it all—to commit to a "full send"—in order to experience that intimacy.

If you choose to dive in (or to dive in deeper), well (1) that's awesome! and (2) I encourage you to continue fostering your relationship with Jesus through the four habits, Mother Mary, and the saints. I also encourage you to get others to dive in with you. This is an adventure that only gets better with others.

There is a never-ending abundance of life that the Lord offers you. Dare to go all in and experience it. As St. Augustine once said, "To fall in love with God is the greatest romance; to seek him the greatest adventure; to find him the greatest human achievement."

Before I left Los Angeles for Colorado, I grabbed my surfboard and went out for one last surf. I dreaded that surf. I'm not good at good-byes, and I was putting this one off for last—my good-bye to the ocean.

The waves were virtually nonexistent that day, a bummer that my last surf would be spent catching ankle biters. I paddled out sans wetsuit because I wanted the water to soak into me. To stain my skin. To become a part of me. The problem with not wearing a wetsuit is that the Pacific is *cold.* Even at its warmest, the water carries a frigid sting. I muscled through the pain for as long as I could because I didn't want to leave the water. I *couldn't* leave the water—but my body could only shake for so long. My hands were looking purple, and my teeth chattered so intensely that I couldn't see straight. I thought I was going to chip a tooth.

Under the click-clack of my teeth, I prayed, "Just one more wave, God. One more." Immediately, my vibrating jaw softened. My vision focused. A sense of stillness and warmth poured over me. I stopped shaking, and my eyes locked onto a beautiful set crawling in from the horizon. A thought popped into my mind: *Go*.

So I went—as the wave arrived, I popped up without hesitation, fully committed. And it was the wave of the day. A beautiful leftie that I rode all the way to shore. The two surfers in the water with me flashed some shakas as I cruised by them. When I hopped off my board, I took off my leash and pounded my chest. I turned around to face the water and take in one more view of the Pacific when another thought popped into my mind: *I have you*.

I believe that was the Lord speaking to me. Whether it actually was his voice or my own thought, it has proven true over the years. The Lord has me. And he promises the same for you. If you close your eyes now, maybe you can hear those same words that were once spoken to me: *Go. I have you.*

**TANNER KALINA** is a Catholic evangelist and works for the National Eucharistic Congress. Kalina speaks at conferences, retreats, and events all across the country, and his videos have accumulated millions of views worldwide. He has appeared in programs for youth through Ascension Press and short video messages on Ascension Presents. He has contributed video projects to EWTN, FOCUS, CatholicMatch, and YDisciple. Kalina cofounded the *Saints Alive* podcast.

Kalina graduated from the University of Texas with a bachelor of arts in radio, television, and film.

He lives with his wife in Denver, Colorado.

www.tannerkalina.com
Facebook: @tanner.kalina
Instagram: @tannerkalina
TikTok: @tannerkalina
YouTube: @tanner.kalina

**KEVIN COTTER** is head of content at Hallow. He previously worked as executive director of The Amazing Parish and senior director of curriculum at FOCUS.

# AVE

AVE MARIA PRESS

Founded in 1865, Ave Maria Press,
a ministry of the Congregation of
Holy Cross, is a Catholic publishing
company that serves the spiritual and
formative needs of the Church and its
schools, institutions, and ministers;
Christian individuals and families; and
others seeking spiritual nourishment.

For a complete listing of titles from

Ave Maria Press

Sorin Books

Forest of Peace

Christian Classics

visit www.avemariapress.com

AVE MARIA PRESS
Notre Dame, IN
A Ministry of the United States Province of Holy Cross